John Moore Capes

The Church of the Apostles

An Historical Inquiry

John Moore Capes

The Church of the Apostles
An Historical Inquiry

ISBN/EAN: 9783337063979

Printed in Europe, USA, Canada, Australia, Japan

Cover: Foto ©Lupo / pixelio.de

More available books at **www.hansebooks.com**

THE CHURCH OF THE APOSTLES

AN HISTORICAL INQUIRY

BY

J. M. CAPES, M.A.

"Put off thy shoes from off thy feet, for the place whereon thou standest is holy ground."—EXODUS iii. 5

LONDON
KEGAN PAUL, TRENCH & CO., 1, PATERNOSTER SQUARE
1886

CONTENTS.

	PAGE
THE AUTHOR TO HIS READERS	vii
CHRONOLOGICAL TABLE ...	xiii

CHAPTER

I. ON THE HISTORICAL STUDY OF THE NEW TESTAMENT	1
II. CHRISTIANITY AND THE ROMAN EMPIRE ...	22
III. THESSALONICA	38
IV. GALATIA	52
V. CORINTH	61
VI. ROME ...	74
VII. EPHESUS	81
VIII. COLOSSE	91
IX. PHILIPPI	97
X. THE EPISTLE TO PHILEMON ...	108
XI. THE EPISTLE TO THE HEBREWS ...	112
XII. THE EPISTLE TO TIMOTHY	122
XIII. THE EPISTLE TO TITUS ...	130
XIV. THE EPISTLE OF ST. JAMES ...	139
XV. THE EPISTLES OF ST. PETER	144
XVI. THE EPISTLES OF ST. JOHN ...	151
XVII. THE EPISTLE OF JUDE	155
XVIII. GENERAL CHARACTER OF THE APOSTOLIC CHURCH ...	157
XIX. THE MILLENNIUM	179
XX. PREDESTINATION AND FREE-WILL	188
XXI. MODERN OBJECTIONS TO A BELIEF IN MIRACLES ...	197

THE AUTHOR TO HIS READERS.

It is with no slight regret that I find my task completed, and nothing now remaining for me but to add a few sentences of farewell to my readers, to be prefixed, according to custom, to my little book. In my opening chapter I have so fully explained the object of the present inquiry, that I have now only to point out the singular value of the Epistles of the New Testament as a storehouse of materials for the study of the life of the first Christians when they were formed into communities after our Lord had left this world.

Every one knows the importance of contemporary documents in the study of the history of any period of the past, and it is the meagreness of such documents in connection with the second century which makes it so difficult for the ecclesiastical historian to trace the stages by which the Christianity of the apostolic period was modified or developed into the Christianity of the patristic period and of the Council of Nice. The mere external symbols of the real life of man are now eagerly sought for, as illustrating his habits, feelings, and opinions. Inscriptions, coins, medals, paintings upon vases, and tablets of burnt clay, are made to yield trustworthy information as to the realities of an existence which once seemed to survive only in name; and the sympathetic imagination supplies the details necessary to fill up the void still remaining, so as to complete the historical picture. These details may sometimes be scarcely warranted by well-proved facts; but they are often in strict harmony with the ascertained laws of human nature itself.

Here, then, in the letters actually written by St. Paul and St. John, by St. Peter and St. James, we have a treasure of instruction for the historian, priceless in value. And its value is enhanced by the fact that these letters were written simply as letters, and with no thought of their being subsequently collected together, and circulated among Christians in all ages, as a manual of faith and conduct. The condition of some local Church, or the circumstances of the time, made it desirable that each letter should be written; and each one has thus a freshness of feeling and a spontaneous fervour of expression which could hardly have been looked for had the writers foreseen the uses to which their writings would be turned in after-times.

A word is necessary as to the order in which the Epistles ought to be read, for whatever purpose they may be consulted. By some unaccountable mischance a general misplacement has taken place in our Bibles, and the reader has nothing to guide him when he wishes to follow St. Paul's Epistles as a reflection of the character of the great apostle. The result has been most unfortunate, and has materially obscured the popular conceptions of the apostle's teaching which have become current in all sections of the Christian Church. I have, I venture to hope, contributed some little help towards the disentanglement of the confusion thus produced; and for the convenience of the reader I have added to this preface a chronological table, showing the dates of the several Epistles, and the places from which they were written, as practically settled by modern criticism. Even if there still remains any doubt as to the exact year in which a few of the Epistles were written and despatched, there is none as to their general order.

The reader will also notice that the places from which the Epistles are here stated to have been written do not always correspond with those given in the New Testament at the end of the several Epistles. How these erroneous statements crept into early copies of the original manuscripts no one now knows. Copyists are proverbially addicted to making explanatory additions to manuscripts entrusted to them for transcription; and in the present case the additions have been made so heedlessly as to be sometimes contradicted in the substance of the letters to which they are appended. The mistakes are not without importance, for they tend to lessen the vividness of our impression of the true character of the Epistles, as the letters of real men to real men and women, showing the influence of the circumstances under which they were written upon the writers themselves.

In the case of St. Paul these mistakes are especially to be regretted. His comprehensive and cultivated intellect, and his sensitive and affectionate heart, made him peculiarly open to impressions from those with whom he was from time to time associated; and his letters often show that the current of his thoughts while writing flowed in directions suggested by the circumstances in which he was placed. Yet, when the reader has found it easy to trace in the Epistle to the Thessalonians the effect of the apostle's observations on the wretchedness and hopelessness of paganism in dissolute Corinth, from which the Epistles to the Thessalonians were really written, he is surprised at being told, at the end of the letters, that they were written from Athens, whose people worshipped the goddess of wisdom and the unknown God, while

Corinth adored Venus, the goddess of pleasure, and practised without shame her voluptuous rites. And so with other Epistles. Wherever there is an error, it tends to obliterate the features of the picture which these letters enable us to draw of the great apostle, and weaken our perception of his wonderful personality, at once so commanding and so irresistibly attractive.

The historical importance of the information thus acquired cannot be overrated. The sentence from the Book of Exodus, which I have placed on my title-page, applies in its measure to the life of the Christians of the apostolic age. That period is emphatically holy ground. No other epoch in the history of Christianity will bear comparison with it in exhibiting the true Christian life, as the result of the life, death, and resurrection of our blessed Lord.

Three circumstances combined to make the Church of the apostles our standard in faith and morals, more trustworthy than any other that the records of Christianity can show to us. Christians were then under the personal guidance of the apostles themselves. The presence of God among them was shown in the frequency with which miraculous gifts were exercised, not only by the apostles, but by many of the private believers; and the sincerity and piety of the believers were tested by persecutions of all kinds, ending frequently in martyrdom.

Whatever, then, have been the changes to which the growth of civilization and the multiplication of conversions have given birth, never again was the Church in so happy a spiritual condition as she enjoyed while the apostles lived; and therefore never again had she equal claims on our respect, our affection, and our reverence. And the more closely and critically these records of her life are examined, the more strikingly will the life of the apostolic period be seen to correspond with the ideal life of Christians in this world which is set forth in the four Gospels themselves.

CHRONOLOGICAL TABLE,

SHOWING THE DATES OF THE EPISTLES, AND THE PLACES FROM WHICH THEY WERE WRITTEN.

	Written from	A.D.
1 Thessalonians	Corinth	52
2 Thessalonians	Corinth	52
Galatians	Corinth	End of 52 or beginning of 53
1 Corinthians	Ephesus	57
Romans	Corinth	End of 57 or beginning of 58
2 Corinthians	Macedonia (perhaps Philippi)	58
Ephesians	Rome	61
Colossians	Rome	62
Philippians	Rome	End of 62 or beginning of 63
Philemon	Rome	End of 62 or beginning of 63
Hebrews	Italy (perhaps Rome)	End of 62 or beginning of 63
1 Timothy	Macedonia	64
Titus	Macedonia	64
2 Timothy	Rome	65
James	Judæa	61
1 Peter	Rome	64
2 Peter	Rome	Beginning of 65
1 John	Unknown (perhaps Ephesus)	68 or early in 69
2 and 3 John	Ephesus	68 or early in 69
Jude	Unknown	63 or 64

THE CHURCH OF THE APOSTLES.

CHAPTER I.

ON THE HISTORICAL STUDY OF THE NEW TESTAMENT.

WHATEVER may be the merits or demerits of the age in which our lot is cast, posterity will certainly be grateful to us for having been the first to comprehend the significance of the great truth that every relic of the past is to be valued as an indication of the characteristic life which gave it birth. Not that past generations were entirely ignorant of this truth, but that it has been reserved for our own to apply it to many subjects to which our ancestors never suspected that it could be applicable.

They were, in a word, antiquaries and collectors, but nothing more. With a childlike simplicity they gathered together all things old and strange, and had no thought of the lessons their collections were capable of teaching. Fossils, minerals, bones of extinct animals, mummies from the Nile, urns from the Catacombs, arrow-heads from caves, jewels from the East, the marbles of Greece, the vases of Etruria, fragments of manuscripts written in characters neither Greek, nor Roman, nor Hebrew, were treasured as rarities, costly and novel, and beyond the understanding of the vulgar mind.

At length a new conception dawned upon the lovers of the relics of the past. They began to suspect that there might be some hidden secret which would give vitality to all these heterogeneous remains. By degrees it came to be imagined that there might be some sort of organic relationship between objects hitherto regarded as utterly dissimilar and unconnected by any common bond of union. Day by day and year by year the new conception grew, and was felt even when not distinctly understood. This was the conception of *life*, as the source of the innumerable varieties in the works accomplished by man, and also in that visible universe in which human intelligence has no part to play.

Thus arose the sciences of comparative physiology, comparative anatomy, and comparative philology; all of them bearing witness to the great truth that a knowledge of the externals of existence is not to be called knowledge at all, unless it leads to the study of that secret life to whose prolific force all the changing phenomena of man's history are due. Hence the increasing conviction that a history of the beliefs of the past is not a history of abstract ideas and speculations, but the history of human beings like ourselves. It is the history of their actual life, rather than a statement of the different views which have from time to time prevailed in respect to the subjects which have interested mankind.

Everywhere are to be seen signs, sometimes trifling but always significant, of this change in the current of the thoughts of educated people. Everywhere there is a recognition of the principle that correctness of knowledge as to the real facts of human life is the first condition of all historical study that is worthy the name. The history of England is something more than a record of the reigns of kings, of battles and sieges, and other public events. If this old-fashioned chronicle of public affairs, which the last century looked upon as history, is not vivified with information as to the habitual life that was lived by the men and women from whom we spring, it is no real history at all.

This is the secret conviction which lies at the root of that laborious examination of the architecture, the dresses, the armour, and weapons of war, which has occupied so much of the attention of the present century. And it is the same with our present studies of all languages.

We no longer regard them as a sort of mysterious invention of grammarians, but as an outgrowth of humanity, the most wonderful of all the implements that have been devised for practical use by the great tool-making animal, man; and as attaining their maturity by certain definite stages of development in harmony with the growth of human nature itself. Thus the science of comparative philology has grown up side by side with the science of comparative physiology; both alike based on the study of life, as such; the one on the emotional and thinking life of man, the other on the facts of the physical life which he shares with the whole animal creation. We should no more think of studying our own language, or the ancient languages of Greece and Rome, apart from the phenomena of the Sanskrit or Semitic languages, than we should think of classifying plants by the Linnæan method of numbering the pistils and stamens of their flowers, or animals by the shape and arrangement of their teeth.

In a like spirit there is a growing tendency to repudiate the habit of regarding the New Testament as a species of magazine of texts, to be employed for controversial purposes; or at the best as a collection of theological documents, originally written and providentially published for the general use of mankind. Christianity, we are now learning to see, is the one great fact in the history of the human race; and neither Christianity itself, nor the human race itself, can be understood apart from one another.

According to the old theory, the New Testament is a kind of concrete entity; an organic whole, to be read without any constant reference to the origin of its separate parts, or to the personal characteristics of its various authors. As far as the Epistles are concerned, no one supposed that they were to be placed as much among the historical as among the doctrinal portions of the sacred volume.

It was through the prevalence of these views that many persons felt as if a severe shock was given to their faith when they learnt that grave doubts were entertained as to the connection of the first three Gospels with the personal disciples of Jesus Christ, whose names they bear. What ground for our faith have we, they asked, if we cannot trust these lives of our Lord as three independant narratives of His life and teaching, written by those who were personally instructed by Himself?

The synoptical theory, however, by degrees made its way, and helped to familiarize men's minds with the conviction that the daily life of the first believers after the departure of Jesus Christ from the world is an elementary fact of the utmost moment, to be taken into account by every one who would understand Christianity itself.

Any honest attempt to realize the actual life of the first disciples at once dissipates the fears of those who imagined that their faith depended upon the maintenance of the old views as to the origin of the Gospels. What, it was asked by thinking people, was the daily existence of the men and women who believed in the Son of Mary as their Redeemer and Teacher? They were for the most part poor and illiterate, and could not read books, even if they had them. Yet they must have possessed some detailed record of the life and teaching of their Master; some narrative of His birth, death, and resurrection. It is simply incredible that no such history was in existence from the first, sufficient for the guidance of the believers. It cannot seriously be maintained that they had no traditional life of Jesus generally current among them, until some of His original followers wrote down in Greek their personal recollections and circulated them as authentic narratives. In other words, the synoptical theory as to the origin of the three first Gospels is in harmony with the facts of the life of the first Christians, as we cannot fail to perceive the moment we study the beginnings of the Christian Church as a history of the real life of human beings like ourselves.

Examining this theory on its merits, we find that it is based upon certain undeniable peculiarities in the three first Gospels themselves. None of them, of course, pretends to record in full detail all the words which Jesus uttered when He instructed His followers, whether in parables or in any other way. Such verbal minuteness would have been as impossible as was unnecessary. What the believers needed was a record of the substance of their Master's teaching, and of the circumstances of His life and death, practically so correct as to be accepted as the groundwork of their faith and conduct. St. John's Gospel concludes with a kind of protest against any other system of narrative as an attempt to do that which was impossible.

In comparing, then, the three first Gospels with one another, the reader is at once struck with a surprising phenomenon. While agreeing substantially as narratives designed for practical guidance, they disagree absolutely in certain details which could hardly have escaped the observation of eye-witnesses; at the same time that they agree verbally in many matters where independent observers, relating the substance of what they had seen and heard, would naturally differ.

What is the explanation of these singular characteristics? The explanation is obvious, as soon as we realize the actual circumstances of the life of the believers. These three Gospels are really three separate versions of the one traditional narrative which was current when they were written. When three different writers undertook to preserve the current narrative, their own personal varieties of feeling and temperament would lead them to record facts and discourses with differences of detail and more or less fulness, as the case might be; while at the same time they preserved with rigid verbal accuracy such portions of the history as they considered to require minute exactness. Each evangelist's narrative was thus a *synopsis* of the previously existing history of the life of Jesus Christ. Accepting this explanation of their origin, the difficulties which have been often caused by the discrepancies in these three Gospels disappear. The authorship of St. John's Gospel is determined by different considerations, into which my present purpose does not make it necessary for me to enter. As to the other three, instead of appearing less trustworthy as narratives, the adoption of the synoptical theory makes them more valuable than before, and we read them with an undoubting conviction that they bring us into the very presence of the incarnate Son of God.

In this spirit of historical criticism I propose to examine the Epistles of St. Paul and of the other writers in the New Testament, with the view of ascertaining what insight they may furnish into the lives, the feelings, and the beliefs of the Christian communities of the apostolic period. A vivid picture of the life of the Patristic period has been drawn by Cardinal Newman in "The Church of the Fathers;" and those who wish to know what were the externals, and incidentally the inner life, of the times subsequent to the conversion of Constantine the Great, will find ample information, mainly in respect to the Christianity of the Latin races, in Dr. Roch's elaborate "The Church of our Fathers."

In the picture which I am now attempting to draw, the personality of one great figure stands out in striking relief. It is that of St. Paul himself; and the more carefully his writings are studied from the historical point of view, the more are we impressed with the heroic greatness and the exquisite charm of character of that wonderful man, appointed by a special revelation to be the apostle of the Gentiles. The more closely his character is examined, the more fitting he appears to have been the one chief exponent of the faith of Christ, both as a preacher and as a writer whose exposition of the doctrines of the Gospel was to be the treasure of Christians in all coming ages.

That, with very few exceptions, St. Paul really wrote the letters attributed to him, there is not the shadow of a doubt. It is as certain that he wrote them as that Julius Cæsar wrote his " Commentaries," or Dante the " Divina Commedia." The authorship of the Epistle to the Hebrews is a question on which critics are divided. Many attribute the Epistle to Apollos, the close friend and disciple of St. Paul. But whoever was its actual writer, its value is undoubted, as illustrating those peculiar elements in the character of the Hebrew converts to the gospel which the writer of the Epistle regarded as requiring special attention. As such, it is one of the most important historical documents of the apostolic period.

It need hardly be added that it is by no means simply as an interesting literary and historical inquiry that I undertake the fulfilment of my present task. An inquiry into the facts of the lives of the early Christian communities is not like an inquiry into the rise and progress of Buddhism, or the origin of the strange religions of Central America. I approach my investigation into the habits and beliefs of the first Christian Churches with a conviction that I am about to study the inmost lives of men who had been, by the will of God, placed in a position different from that of all the rest of mankind. They had learnt truths of which the wisest and most learned were ignorant. Their chief teacher had been himself the subject of a supernatural interposition, which had changed his whole nature, and he had subsequently been miraculously instructed on many details of the matters which he communicated to his followers.

In examining these letters, therefore, I begin by recognizing the divine origin of the religion which St. Paul taught. Christianity, I see, is the one great fact in the history of the world. We, who are involved in the mystifications of modern popular talk, do not always understand this historical aspect of the religion in which we have been brought up. We regard it as a collection of doctrines and precepts, supported by an ingenious arrangement of texts and authorities, whose miraculous elements have become things of the past, and have no practical bearing upon our everyday existence.

The Christianity of the early Christians was of a different kind. It was essentially a religion which recognized the reality of supernatural agencies, continued without interruption from the time when Jesus was born in Bethlehem. It seems unprofitable, therefore, to inquire into the history of St. Paul's converts until we have satisfied ourselves that no valid reason exists for disbelieving the reality of that supernatural life which St. Paul assumed to be involved in the fundamental constitution of Christianity itself. The most modern speculations on this momentous question will be discussed in a subsequent chapter; but it may be well to anticipate at once the difficulties which in earlier times have presented themselves to serious thinkers who see in all supernatural events an infraction of the laws of the universe.

Were, then, the miracles recorded in the Gospels and the Acts of the Apostles in themselves impossible? That they were in themselves, strictly speaking, impossible, cannot be supposed by any thinking mind which believes in the existence of an Almighty God, and His power over all things that He has created.

But the notion of the impossibility of miracles is supplemented by another theory, at first sight more plausible, but which disappears on close examination. All miracles, it is argued, are violations of the principle of the inviolability of law, as the expression of the eternal and unchangeable nature of God Himself. Undoubtedly this is so. But the objection has no bearing upon the reality of the Christian miracles, which are based upon the fact that man's nature is twofold. If there is a God, and we are capable of any actions of a moral or immoral kind, it follows, as a necessary consequence, that we are responsible to Him for all our conduct. If our nature were in all respects identical with that of the brutes, matters would be different. Our interests would be confined to the affairs of the present life and to the laws which regulate the visible universe.

But, inasmuch as our nature has its moral and spiritual as well as its corporeal relations, it is subject to a twofold system of law; the laws of the invisible universe as well as those of the visible; and farther, we must recognize in the eternal and unchanging nature of the Godhead the cause of the permanent reign of law in the unseen as well as in the things that are seen. When, therefore, in the furtherance of our moral discipline, it pleases God to interfere with the regular course of the laws which regulate visible things, we are not to regard Him as violating the first principle of the uniformity of law in itself. On the contrary, He is breaking into the inviolability of visible law, in order to teach us His presence as the Author of that higher law which has reference to the nobler portion of our being; that is, our moral and spiritual nature. When an Infant is born from a virgin mother, the laws of the material universe are interrupted, but not those of the spiritual universe, and man learns that in a true and real sense the new-born Child is the Redeemer, the Son of the Most High, come to save him from his sins.

When, then, I find, in more than one of St. Paul's

letters, that he speaks of certain supernatural gifts, possessed by members of the community to which he is writing, my conviction of the inviolability of law, as such, is not interfered with. The phenomena spoken of are simply phenomena; wonderful, indeed, but not incredible. I do not doubt that they really existed, precisely as St. Paul described them. I am not driven, in bewilderment, to take refuge in the supposition that St. Paul was either so simple-minded and credulous as to mistake his own illusions for actual facts, or so dishonest as to suppress his conviction that the supposed miraculous gifts were a dream or an imposture. I accept the statement in his Epistles as the historical record of real events, which were altogether in harmony with the promises made by our Lord during His lifetime.

If I am asked whether I have ever been personally cognisant of the exercise of such powers by Christians at the present day, I reply that I have not; and I add without hesitation, that if I did witness any professed miracle, I should, of course, be astonished, and I should try its reality by the severest tests; but I should not hold that it was necessarily a delusion.

As a Christian, I am convinced that I am living in the midst of an invisible and supernatural world, which is as truly an objective reality as the things which I touch and see and hear. It is real, because God Himself is real. To this unseen reality I myself have access by means of faith and prayer;

and I am not an unreasoning fanatic because I habitually ask God to give me many things which I desire, and believe that He often grants my requests. This, I say, is what every intelligent Christian holds; and if it is objected that such a belief is equivalent to an assertion that our prayers work miracles, I reply that I am not to be frightened by words from exercising the privileges which as a Christian I possess. If any person imagines that it is preposterous to suppose that he or I, or any one, should have the power of communicating with the Eternal God, and by a mere silent prayer to induce Him to make some alteration in the course of the visible universe, the answer is obvious. God is everywhere, and to Him nothing is little and nothing is great. The trifles of daily life and the shock of empires are in His eyes alike deserving of the attention of His wisdom and the control of His omnipotence; and that man best does his duty to his fellow-men, and walks with surest step through the tangled paths of this visible world whose vision of unseen things is most clear and uninterrupted, and whose look is most steadily fixed, not upon his own miserable inward self, but upon that living Presence in which he lives and moves and has his being.*

Such being our own daily life, we study the details of the Epistles in the New Testament with intense interest, but not with any very great surprise. If it is sometimes difficult to picture to ourselves

* See chap. xxi.

states of society such as existed in Thessalonica, or Corinth, or Rome, or Ephesus, it is not so much on account of their religious peculiarities as because the general conditions of their civilization were so unlike our own. To superficial observers old times seem to be specially distinguished from the present by differences in language, in architecture and furniture, in dress, and in customs of eating and drinking. These things, however, were only the externals of ancient life, as they are the externals of our own.

The differences between our lives and those of the Christians of the apostolic period lay far deeper than any mere investigation of the externals of civilization can reveal. The influence of Christian morality has left such an impression upon our personal, social, and domestic ideas, that we find it difficult to realize the tone of thought and feeling which prevailed in all classes of men and women brought up under the accumulated influences of hundreds and thousands of years of heathenism or unmodified Judaism. Looking back upon our own English life, such as it was some two or three centuries ago, any trustworthy contemporary record of its features convinces us that our ancestors of those days were in some respects singularly unlike ourselves. Still more strikingly is this the case when the retrospect is carried into foreign countries, and we are brought face to face with their private life, such as it existed some eight or ten generations ago. We are sometimes so startled by what we see to have been their habitual modes of thought, that we are almost tempted to ask whether these people were literally of the same flesh and blood as ourselves.

Imagine, then, what the citizens of Rome, or Corinth, or Ephesus were, before one Christian idea had penetrated into the chaotic compound of notions engendered by Oriental, Greek, and Roman mythologies, complicated with the incessant conflicts of political strife, in which our modern ideas of right and wrong, and of the relations of the sexes, had no place.

Side by side with these pagan elements was the power of what I have called unmodified Judaism, when the Christian ideas which have now so largely modified the ancient Judaism were unknown to the Jew of Judæa, of Italy, or of Asia, except as objects of his aversion or contempt. The Gospel histories show distinctly to what a small extent the popular Judaism of the day had shared in such civilization as the world then knew. There seems to have been only one important element in social life in which the Jews had changed for the better. They had, as far as can be gathered from the Gospels, given up the practice of polygamy, and the recognized concubinage of the patriarchs seems to have been laid aside. In this abolition of polygamy they simply acted upon the ideas which were current in the nations of civilized Europe, Greece and Rome alike having come to the conclusion that the practice of polygamy was inconsistent with the well-being of society. But the Jews of the time were still lax on the subject of divorce, while, so far from having made any approach towards the fundamental Christian doctrine of the forgiveness of injuries their natures were as hard and cruel as they had ever been. To-day, few cultivated Jews would assert that the Lord's Prayer addresses Almighty God in a manner which is alien to his Hebrew feelings; but this is the result of that indirect influence which Christianity has exercised in so many quarters where its light has shone, undarkened by gross corruptions. The Jew of eighteen centuries ago was a being as little like the half-Christianized Jew, with whose merits we are now familiar, as the voluptuous heathen of Corinth was unlike the philosophic moralists of Athens or the ascetics of Brahmanism in India.

Imagine, then, I say, what life must have been in those old days, and we shall recognize the difficulty of understanding it, whether in its lights or its shadows, as it was lived by the Christian converts in the time of the apostles.

I should add a few words of a personal nature, which will perhaps not lessen the interest which the reader may feel in the attempt I am now making to enable him to realize the actual life of the early Christian Churches. Most men, as they advance in years, grow more and more conscious of the unsatisfying character of that strange development of religious civilization in which we now find ourselves. All things seem in confusion, and almost unreal and dream-like. There is a vast amount of good intention and good feeling among us, notwithstanding the violence of ecclesiastical and political partisanship. But sensible persons, as they grow old, learn to dislike partisanship with a cordial dislike. They know that there are few subjects which are not many-sided and complex, and on which wise and honest minds may not differ. Still, though they can never be vehement partisans, their human hearts long for sympathy with living beings like themselves. Those who are young and eager do not understand this desire for sympathy on the part of the old. They do not understand why men and women who seem to belong to a dead generation cannot content themselves with the interests of the past, and satisfy their vain cravings with abstract reasonings and critical studies, especially of a devout description.

Yet it is really because certain old books correspond to this desire for personal knowledge and sympathy that they hold their place among the great masterpieces of literature of all ages, and have retained their charm for successive generations of men.

Such is that most perfect of all books outside the sacred Scriptures, the "Imitation [or, 'Following'] of Christ." Its authorship, as critics are aware, is attributed to two different persons, placed in very different circumstances — Thomas à Kempis, a member of a Flemish monastery; and Gerson, a French ecclesiastic filling a distinguished post, and engaged in the active controversies of a stirring age. But whichever of the two men was the writer of the wonderful book, every person who now reads it feels that he is not merely following the guidance of an incomparable spiritual teacher, but is holding communion with a living human being, no longer present in this world, but still speaking to us, heart to heart, as a personal friend, in his saintly pages.

And this is just the kind of sympathy which is to be found in the lives of the apostolic Christians when we have learnt to realize their characteristic features. Here, at any rate, were people into whose daily struggles we can throw our whole hearts without fear of indulging in vulgar partisanship. Granting that at times some of them fell into grievous sin, and that they were occasionally misled by opinions whose foolishness is now manifest, still they were the uncompromising servants of Jesus Christ, who lived for Him and often died for Him. In the study of their daily customs, their difficulties, their occasional failures, their hopes, and their victories, we live their lives over again; we are at home among them, with a brotherly sympathy that satisfies us when we are most lonely amidst the crowd of nineteenth-century combatants.

The peculiar character of St. Paul's mind materially lessens any difficulty that might be felt in reproducing the life of the early Christian Churches from the letters which he addressed to them. I do not mean his personal and moral nature, which will come out in strong relief as we examine his writings in detail, but his intellectual nature. This was eminently of the practical type, as distinguished from the purely speculative. However abstract are the subjects that he treats, he invariably contemplates them in their relation to human action, and the capacity of the human intellect to turn them to profit in its efforts to comprehend Divine mysteries.

This is especially notable in his method of treating the subject of the Divine foreknowledge, and of election and predestination. The subject, as is well known to every one who is familiar with it, is in itself a metaphysical question, involving ideas as obscure as they are profound. How to reconcile our conceptions of liberty and necessity, of God's foreknowlege of events with man's freedom of action in human affairs, is a problem which has proved insoluble to the keenest intellects in all ages, though it has never ceased to perplex and excite the serious thinkers of every race.

In reality the problem is necessarily insoluble. It involves conceptions of the operations of the Divine mind which are simply beyond the reach of any human intelligence. "Canst thou by searching find out God?" says the Scripture; and the absurdity of the attempt is demonstrated when we try to frame a distinct idea of that which is in itself infinite without falling into self-contradictions. Foreknowledge and predestination being essentially the acts of a Being whose modes of action imply powers which are in themselves incomprehensible to us, any attempt to reconcile them theoretically with the free agency of beings whose every action is thus foreknown must result in the invention of mere highsounding phrases, as destitute of intelligible meaning as the empty vibrations of a drum.*

When St. Paul introduces the subject, as he does in writing to the Romans, he never treats it as a matter of interesting philosophical and theological speculation, involving serious difficulties, to be approached with due caution and with a careful balancing of apparently contradictory propositions. He views the doctrine of election as a simple truth, having certain definite practical bearings upon the life of the believer. He points out the consequences which it involves, and the several steps in the process of perfecting the true saint, by which God carries out His own predestinating will. The contrast between St. Paul's method and that of writers of the speculative school is complete, and deepens our impression of his marvellous personal fitness for the work to which he was called when God made him the apostle of the Gentiles.

* See chap. xx.

CHAPTER II.

CHRISTIANITY AND THE ROMAN EMPIRE.

I. In attempting to picture to ourselves the actual life of the Christian believers of the apostolic period, our attention is at once arrested by two great facts —the vast and homogeneous organization of the Roman empire, and the absence of any complete and vigorous organization in the spiritual kingdom which was to prove its overthrow.

The fifteenth chapter of the Acts of the Apostles records the first steps which were taken to lay a basis for the general organization of the Christian Churches, and to secure uniformity in faith and practice. This was nearly twenty years after the death of our Lord. The apostles and elders then met in council at Jerusalem, in order to decide upon the pretensions which had been put forward by the Jewish party among the believers after the conversion of the Gentiles had been admitted as coming within the scope of the command given by Jesus Christ to the apostles.

Defeated in their exclusive claims, the Jewish

party devised a new scheme for fettering the consciences of the Gentiles, whose conversion they could not prevent. They insisted that the observance of the whole Mosaic law, including the rite of circumcision, was obligatory upon all Christians, whether of Jewish or Gentile origin. The agitation caused by this assertion, and the pertinacity with which it was urged, were so great that the apostles and elders assembled in council at Jerusalem to decide the matter. On the proposition of Peter, who had himself opposed the admission of Gentiles to the privileges of Christians till he was convinced by a vision, the pretensions of the Judaising party were formally condemned, and messengers were sent to communicate the decision to the disturbed districts.

II. In the mean time Divine Providence was preparing a new supernatural force, which would exercise the most momentous influence in the conversion of the world and in the administration of the affairs of the Church. When the first martyr, Stephen, was murdered by the Jews in Jerusalem, a young man, named Saul, stood by, exulting in the crime, and thinking that the murderers were doing God service. This young man, afterwards called Paul, was a Jew of the tribe of Benjamin, of good family, and belonging to the sect of the Pharisees. He was also a Roman citizen, having inherited the privileges of citizenship from his father. It is to be noted that the personal rights of citizenship, when inherited, were greater than those connected with a citizenship conferred upon an individual foreigner. Upon this peculiarity in the Roman law the subsequent fortunes of Paul turned on a certain great occasion, and through the operation of this privilege the destinies of the Christian Church were materially affected.

Saul, though a Hebrew of the Hebrews, was born at Tarsus, a city in Cilicia, a place of much cultivation, where he was educated in all the accomplishments of the time, learning to speak both Greek and Latin. According to the custom which prevailed among the wealthy Jews, he learnt a mechanical trade, and was able, if necessary, to support himself by tent-making. When his home education was finished, he was placed under the care of Gamaliel, a rabbi of high reputation at Jerusalem. From Gamaliel he acquired a full knowledge of the written and unwritten traditions of the Jewish law. His full knowledge of the writings of the Old Testament might have been acquired before he became the pupil of Gamaliel.

He was endowed, besides, with a bodily constitution of extraordinary vigour, and united sensitiveness of feeling to tenacity and courage to an unusual degree. He was passionately devoted to his race and all its laws and customs, and he threw himself with ardour into the growing conflict between Judaism and the religion of Jesus, of which latter he knew little or nothing.

After witnessing the hideous death of Stephen, and exasperated by the martyr's faith and constancy, Saul proceeded to take active steps for stopping the progress of the new creed. The pretence that the Christians were disloyal to the Roman power enabled the Jews to obtain warrants for their apprehension, the execution of which was entrusted to Saul, who started at once for Damascus.

On his way Jesus spoke to him, without showing Himself to his bodily eyes. He had nearly reached the city when he was startled by a sudden light blazing before him. He fell to the ground, but at once he knew that he was in the presence of a Divine manifestation. "Who art Thou, Lord?" he asked. A voice replied, "I am Jesus, whom thou persecutest. It is hard for thee to kick against the pricks." The words pierced the heart of the young man, and he understood that he had been the victim of his own passionate self-will, and that the persecuted Christians were the only followers of the one true God. His whole nature instantly submitted without reserve, and he was directed to go into Damascus, where he would learn what he was to do. The voice then was silent; and Saul, who had been blinded by the light, was led into the city by his attendants, who had heard the voice, but seen nothing. In Damascus he was found by Ananias, a disciple, who had been supernaturally instructed to meet him, and by whom, after his sight was miraculously restored, he was baptized.

III. And thus Jesus Christ prepared the new apostle, who was to be pre-eminently the teacher of the Gentile world, and to stand face to face with the gigantic organization of the Roman empire. From this time the history of the conflict between the power of Rome and the spiritual kingdom of Christ is, to a large extent, a history of the life of St. Paul, and a description of the lives of the various Christian communities to whom he wrote the numerous letters collected together in the New Testament. It seems probable that all the letters he thus wrote have been preserved. In the communities to whom they were addressed there would naturally exist the greatest anxiety for their preservation; and, when supplemented by the Epistles written by a few of the original apostles, they thus supply ample materials for a fairly complete narrative of the daily existence of the first Christians and of the influences which the Roman empire brought to bear upon their lives and fortunes. They have only to be studied without prejudice or controversial bias in order to enable us to realize the true nature of that conflict with the world in which Christians are necessarily engaged, and will be engaged, as long as the world shall last. Such a picture of the energetic life of "the Church of the Apostles" must be not only in the highest degree interesting, but will supply an important element towards a thorough comprehension of the history of Christian doctrine, and of that growth of

Christian practices and modes of expression which has been the result of the undying vitality of the Church.

It is instructive, too, as has been already said, to us who are born in an age when it is comparatively easy to live a Christian life, to recall the terrible nature of the strife which was maintained by our spiritual forefathers eighteen centuries ago, when the circumstances of civilized society were so little like those of our own time, and a sharp line marked the followers of Jesus Christ from those who were His enemies.

IV. In the fifty-second year after the birth of our Lord, when the earliest of St. Paul's letters, that which he sent to the Thessalonians from Corinth, is believed to have been written, the Roman empire was master of nearly all the thickly-peopled parts of Europe and of a considerable portion of Asia, to say nothing of the footing which it had gained on the northern shores of Africa. And thus it is, that, when we trace the features of the life of the Church in the apostolic age, we find everywhere the signs of that peculiar influence which Rome exercised over the races subject to her sway. It was through that unity of government which was characteristic of her system that the first preachers of Christianity were able to travel to and fro at their pleasure, with little or no hindrance. The general use of the Greek language as a means of communication, like French in modern times, was another effect of the Roman unity of administration, whose importance it is difficult to overrate when the apostles came to write to the converts whom they made. Even when writing to the Jewish Christians in general, the author of the Epistle to the Hebrews wrote in Greek, with no apology for using a language which might be supposed strange in their ears.

V. Again, it was through the action of the Roman system that large numbers of Jews were already settled in many of the cities to which the apostles carried the tidings of the gospel. Hence it was that the fundamental doctrine of Christianity, which asserted that the gospel was designed for all mankind without distinction of nation, was at once made a matter of vehement practical discussion, sometimes embittered with all the acrimony which an ancient and narrow-minded people like the Jews were capable of feeling.

VI. Another important element in the practical application of the teaching of Jesus Christ was the result of the peculiar temperament of the Jewish race when brought into collision with the peculiar temperament of Rome and of all persons whose natures were moulded by her example. To some extent the subtle, passionate, and poetic Greek nature had modified the hard, straightforward, and relentless Roman nature; but it had not seriously lessened its resoluteness and love for practical thoroughness, as distinct from intellectual refinements and fondness for artistic propriety and beauty of form.

"*Græcia capta*," said the Roman poet, "*ferum victorem cepit, et artes intulit agresti Latio.*" But though conquered Greece thus made her conqueror captive, it was her arts that she introduced into rude and rustic Latium. The essence of the Roman nature remained unchanged, and the more so, as it was at first almost exclusively the higher ranks of Roman society which felt the influence of Greek culture.

In the national stubbornness of the Jewish race Rome met with her equal in determination and obstinacy. The old type of the Hebrew temperament remains, in truth, but little altered to this hour. Eighteen centuries have passed away, but the Jew is still very like what he was when he endured all the horrors of the siege of Jerusalem under the Emperor Titus, not twenty years after St. Paul wrote his Epistles to the Thessalonians.

Thus it was that the early controversies concerning the doctrines and morals of Christianity were carried on by two races unlike any others in the world, and their issues were determined by men to whom feebleness and vacillation were known only to be regarded with contempt.

VII. What was the prevalent morality of Roman society when the apostles preached the moral law of Christ it is not easy to determine. Its corruptness has sometimes been exaggerated by Christian writers, who have thus thrown needless difficulties in the way of those who wish to picture to themselves the details of the life of the different communities to whom the apostolical Epistles were addressed. A correct estimate of the notions on right and wrong which prevailed in Roman society must not be looked for in the denunciations of a professed satirist like Juvenal, any more than in a poem like the "Æneid," in which Virgil makes one of his chief personages express his belief in a doctrine scarcely distinguishable from the Catholic doctrine of purgatory, or in the exquisite burst of feeling in which Tacitus speculates on the eternal destiny of the virtuous Agricola.

A more trustworthy exponent of the recognized tone of Roman morals is to be found in Horace; gentlemanly, Epicurean, and almost refined in his tastes; a thorough man of the world, as we understand the form when we describe a person to whom the Christian ideas of purity and humility are empty phrases. There is little doubt that in Horace we have a correct type of old Roman life, as it existed, with occasional exceptions, in the cities of Italy, Greece, and Asia Minor. Corinth, it is true, was pre-eminently a city of pleasure, like Paris or Bucharest to-day. But it is a mistake to suppose that gross vice was always found flourishing in the Gentile world in apostolic times, or that no virtues were to be found in the popular heathenism. The figures of the Sibyls on the ceiling of the Sistine Chapel in the Vatican, sitting side by side with the Hebrew prophets, are not simply the creation of a painter's daring imagination. They embody the historical fact, that in the pagan world there were many men and women to whom the preaching of the gospel came as a revelation ardently longed for by the deepest desires of their hearts, and clearing up the difficulties which were bowing their intellects to the ground.

VIII. The internal condition of the Roman empire was, in truth, the chief element in that "fulness of time," of which St. Paul speaks in his Epistle to the Galatians, when it was intended in the counsels of God that His Son should be born of a woman. We cannot but believe that by the phrase "the fulness of time," and similar expressions, St. Paul meant that from all eternity God had fixed a certain date for the appearance of the Messiah, and that when that year had arrived Jesus would be born.

The birth of Jesus at the exact period when it took place was really an illustration of that mystery of Omnipotence by which God accomplishes its purposes through the agency of the free will of man. When the peculiar character of any individual man makes him specially fit for some purpose which it is the will of God to accomplish, that individual man is placed in the circumstances suited to the work which he has to do.

The study of St. Paul's Epistles places in the clearest light this method of adapting means to ends which is characteristic of the Divine government. If ever there was a man personally fitted for a certain work, the great apostle of the Gentiles was that man. Nevertheless, the conversion of the Gentiles was not a question of biography, just as the date of the birth of the Messiah was not a question of chronology. It was, to use a modern term, a question of evolution. Mary was made the mother of Jesus because the Jewish nation and the Gentile world had reached precisely that stage of growth which most completely harmonized with the hidden intentions of the Almighty Lord of all.

Thus it is that the unprecedented circumstances of human society, under the sway of Roman administrative imperialism, supplied the soil in which it was the will of God that the teachings of the gospel should grow freely and flourish. These circumstances do not, as Gibbon and other sceptical writers would have us believe, account for the spread of Christianity as a purely human invention. They simply illustrate the universal method by which God governs the world which He has created.

IX. On the correctness and completeness of the conception that we can form of the influence exercised by this Roman power upon the first Christians depends, as I have implied, the correctness of our estimate of the life of the apostolic Churches, viewed as societies of human beings, of flesh and blood like our own. To frame this conception, it is not enough to recall the language and literature of Rome, or the costumes and architecture of Pompeii and Herculaneum, now disinterred from the ashes and the lava where they have lain buried almost since the days of St. Paul. It is not enough to recall the public and political events of the apostolic age. These things are only the dry bones of the past, like those which the prophet saw in his vision in the valley of Jehoshaphat. A fruitful imagination must make these dry bones live again, and clothe them with the flesh and blood, with the beating hearts and flashing eyes of breathing and moving men and women. Then we shall understand what life really was at Rome, and Corinth, and Ephesus, and Philippi. We shall comprehend what the gospel was—a vitalizing force rather than a system of theological propositions—because we shall sympathize with the human beings who received it, and sit with them when they talked with one another, and walk with them when they went into the fields to meditate. This is really to understand Christianity, as well as to follow the course of ecclesiastical history. It is to realize the truth, not only that all races of men are of one nature, but that the saints of God are all one, united in one Lord and Saviour, Jesus Christ.

X. In thus recalling the practical life of the apostolic Christians in the midst of the influences of Roman opinion, one circumstance, at first sight inexplicable, stands out with marked prominence. This is the universal hostility of the philosophic systems of the time towards the doctrines of the gospel. Again and again we find St. Paul referring to it, and writing as if he regarded the antagonism as perfectly natural. In the strongest terms he not only warns the believers against the subtle influences of the philosophies of the heathen world, but he assumes it as a necessary element in their lives that philosophy should not predispose men's minds to accept Christianity as of Divine origin.

How was this? it will be asked. What was the nature of those philosophic theories which thus had the effect of creating an actual antagonism to the gospel, instead of leading men to recognize in it the solution of that mystery of existence which all wise men had been attempting to explain?

The philosophic systems which had taken possession of the Roman intellect were really only two, both of them practical rather than speculative—the systems of Epicurus and of Zeno the Stoic. Epicurus taught that the gods do not trouble themselves about human affairs, and that the wisest men are those who make this life a period of tranquil enjoyment. Zeno held different views, and was the master of nearly all the nobler minds of Rome. Wisdom, he taught them, consists in self-conquest, and in rising superior to all the pains and anxieties of life. The Emperor Marcus Aurelius has left us a remarkable picture of the power of the Stoic philosophy in his "Meditations," or "Diary." His natural character was singularly refined and elevated, and his opinions on questions of right and wrong approach the morality of the gospel. The work is really a daily record of his own inner life, and exhibits him as a model of the virtues to which heathenism could attain in an essentially Roman nature.

The more speculative philosophies of Plato and Aristotle had less attraction for this Roman nature. What would have been their effect in predisposing men's minds towards the gospel, or against it, we have few materials for judging; but it seems likely that their tendencies would on the whole have been anti-Christian. What we have to note is the undoubted fact, that even the austere morality of Stoicism did not lead those who acted upon it to recognize in the great Teacher of the Sermon on the Mount a Master whose claims to be accepted as a Divine Lawgiver demanded the most respectful attention. How is this to be accounted for?

XI. The explanation is at hand. No Greek philosopher ever formed a conception of the truth that profound personal humility is the only basis of all moral goodness. Every attempt at being wise or good which rests on self-reliance is an utter failure. Hence, when the philosophers heard of the Christian doctrine of the self-humiliation of the Son of God, they scorned it as a preposterous absurdity. When paganism had dreamed of any sort of incarnation of its divinities, it had invented fables whose revolting character is thinly veiled, but not disguised, by the exquisite poetry of the "Iliad" and the "Odyssey," and the dignity and loveliness of the sculptures of Phidias and Praxiteles. These fables of popular mythology were, indeed, treated as fables by the philosophic intellect; but they were the creations of minds akin to itself, and were thought to be poetic and harmless, and even useful for the multitude.

Conceive, then, the amazement of the haughty philosophic Greek or Roman, when he heard from the lips of St. Paul or of some Christian convert any expressions corresponding with the doctrine of the Incarnation, as set forth in the Epistle to the Philippians: "Let this mind be in you, which was also in Christ Jesus: who, being in the form of God, thought it not robbery to be equal with God: but made Himself of no reputation, and took upon Him the form of a servant, and was made in the likeness of men : and being found in fashion as a man, He humbled Himself, and became obedient unto death, even the death of the cross. Wherefore also God hath highly exalted Him, and given Him the name which is above every name : that at the name of Jesus every knee should bow, of things in heaven, and things on earth, and things under the earth ; and that every tongue should confess that Jesus Christ is Lord, to the glory of God the Father." *

To our philosopher the very phraseology of these sublime sentences would be but imperfectly intelligible, but he would understand enough of their general drift to kindle his passionate anger or his contemptuous scorn. And in his private intercourse

* Phil. ii. 5-11.

with those who bowed their knees to Jesus, he would direct his keenest sarcasms to undermine their faith, and when he failed to undermine it, he would try so to distort it with his insinuations, that all its simplicity and purity would be gone.

What wonder, then, that we find St. Paul again and again warning the believers against the influences of the philosophy of men, and teaching them that the doctrines of the cross must necessarily appear foolishness to the wise men of the world? And the more closely the matter is examined, the more distinctly we recognize the necessary antagonism of the ancient philosophies to a creed which rested on a belief in the incarnation of the Eternal Son, not for His own gratification, but in order to save from its sins a helpless and miserable world.

CHAPTER III.

THESSALONICA.

I. On the southern coast of Macedonia, close to the great military road leading from Dyrrachium to Byzantium, and overlooking the waters of the Ægean Sea, stood an ancient city, whose name is familiar to modern readers, from its importance as a strategical and commercial centre, and as an object of open desire on the part of those nations who are now eager to share in those remains of the old Roman empire which have been for centuries under the rule of the Mahometan Turks. Salonica, once Thessalonica, was associated with one of the most momentous events which have marked the history of mankind, nearly five hundred years before the birth of Jesus Christ. From the summit of the hills above its bay, Xerxes looked down upon the vast fleet bearing the hordes with which he hoped to crush the power of civilized Greece, and rule with autocratic tyranny over tribes of conquered slaves. Before these five centuries had well expired, the last great monarchy of the heathen world was already showing signs of that silent undermining which was destined to break it in pieces, and rear in its place a new monarchy, the spiritual kingdom of the Son of Mary, the maiden of Bethlehem.

When the news of the birth, death, and resurrection of Jesus was first brought to Thessalonica, it was still an important and thriving place, distinguished from other cities on the seaboard of Asia Minor by its social and political reputation, as the residence of the Roman governor of Macedonia. Its inhabitants in general inherited much of that force of character through which Philip, the Macedonian king, had overpowered the resistance of the Athenian soldiery, though inspired by the fiery eloquence of the heroic Demosthenes. In the two letters which St. Paul wrote to his converts at Thessalonica, it is easy to discover tokens of that simplicity and thoroughness of nature, still surviving among them, which were to be noted in the Macedonian troops of Philip and his son Alexander, and not in the brave though vanquished people of Athens and the Greeks of the Peloponnesus. Certainly there was something in them which called into play all the emotions of St. Paul's affectionate heart. Again and again he returns to the subject, and tells them of the comfort he found in thinking of their steadfastness, and how he habitually prayed for their welfare. And all this comes out so spontaneously, that we cannot fail to understand what sort of people these Thessalonian Christians were; how simple-minded, generous, and unaffected. Nor are we surprised when we read what the apostle says about the influence which their example exercised upon the believers in other parts of the country. Clearly, there were few local Churches which cost him so little anxiety, and which exhibited to their heathen friends and kinsfolk so striking an exemplification of those peculiarities of the Christian character which were at once so strange and so winning in the eyes of intelligent paganism.

II. It was about twenty years after the death of Jesus Christ that it was rumoured in the market-place and on the shore of the bay of Thessalonica that a visit was expected from the wonderful man, about whom the inhabitants had heard such conflicting reports. It was said that he was a Jew of high caste, once a persecutor of the Christians, but now the fearless advocate of the claims of the crucified Jesus. What he specifically taught, and what kind of man he was, no one seemed to know, except vaguely. What was certain was, that wherever he and his companions had been, an indescribable movement of popular feeling had been the result of their speaking. Paul, as he was generally called, notwithstanding his Jewish origin, made friends and enemies everywhere, his enemies accusing him of turning the world upside down, and his friends attaching themselves to him with inexplicable fervour. If only from curiosity to see and hear so extraordinary a person, all classes in Thessalonica were more or less excited by the news that he was to appear among them.

III. Soon it was known that he had arrived, and that on the next day he would speak in the synagogue which belonged to a community of Jews settled in the city. Of the crowd that came together to hear him, few can have been prepared for his exact appearance when he presented himself. He was not a man of commanding presence, and those who expected a display of the arts of the popular orator or the professed rhetorician were disappointed. Those who could read deeper than the surface saw a man apparently of good education, animated by a sense of personal dignity, all the more remarkable because of his absolute absorption in the subject on which he spoke. Tradition has not preserved any account of the peculiar quality of St. Paul's voice; but from the knowledge of his character which we gather from his various Epistles, it cannot be doubted that the tenderness of an unusually sweet and loving disposition was apparent in every sentence that he uttered. Recalling the scene in that provincial synagogue, as he stood before his Jewish and Gentile hearers, and told them that the crucified Jesus was the Son of the Eternal God, we can realize the deep silence that fell upon the assembly, unbroken except by the sob or sigh of some listener, touched to the quick by the tidings of the salvation which Paul offered to all men in the name of God.

At length the speaker ceased, and the listeners dispersed. On the two following sabbaths Paul repeated his reasonings, and their effect was not long in showing itself. Of the Jews not many were convinced. Their proud, narrow, unspiritual nationalism blinded their minds to the apostle's arguments. It was in vain that he showed them that the Messiah whom their Scriptures promised was One who would suffer and die in order to set up a kingdom not of this world. With few exceptions, they were unconscious of that sense of sin and misery which leads the intellect to acquiesce in a spiritual interpretation of the Old Testament promises of a conquering Deliverer. Of the Gentiles, on the contrary, not a few were moved by Paul's argument. Ignorant though they were of the writings of the Hebrew psalmists and prophets, many among them were overpowered by a sense of helplessness and misery which the speculations of the most enlightened paganism failed to explain. Frequent conversations with the apostle himself and with Silas his companion confirmed the impressions made upon these pious Gentiles, and strengthened the resolutions of those who might be disposed to waver.

Then quickly the natural bitterness of Judaism broke out into personal hostility. The unconverted Jews stirred up the passions of a mob of the lowest inhabitants of the city, always ready for a riot; and Paul and Silas were dragged before the magistrates, and accused of designs against the Roman authority.

It was the standing charge against the followers of Christ, as it had been the charge urged against Himself, as false as it was malicious. But it answered the purpose of those who got up the cry; and the magistrates of Thessalonica being no wiser or more honest than Pontius Pilate, the friends of Paul and Silas saw that there was no way of securing their safety if they remained in the city, and they accordingly sent them away by night.

From Thessalonica Paul went to Berea, but the malignity of his Thessalonian Jewish enemies followed him thither, and, with Silas, he was compelled to fly. He visited Athens and Corinth, and from Corinth he wrote his letters to the converts whom he had left behind at Thessalonica. Before writing the first of the two letters he had sent his disciple Timothy to see them, and to bring him confidential information concerning their spiritual condition under the trying circumstances in which they were placed, aggravated as were their difficulties by his own enforced flight from the city and neighbourhood. Timothy brought back with him a most cheering account of their steadfastness and faith, and of the affection which they cherished for Paul himself.

IV. On receiving this report, the apostle, who was then at Corinth, wrote and despatched his First Epistle to the Thessalonians, which, as far as is known, is the first letter that he ever wrote to any of his converts. It is singularly interesting, and, when read in connection with the second letter, which was not long in following, it enables us to realize distinctly the life which was being led by the Christian believers in the midst of their still unconverted fellow-townsmen. Quite as much as any of St. Paul's Epistles, it is stamped with the marks of that individuality of character which distinguished him, and which was one of the secrets of his wonderful success among persons of every variety of nationality and cultivation. It was this profoundly sympathetic heart of the great apostle that made him a master among men, wherever he carried the tidings of that Divine love which had won over his own heart, and changed the persecutor of the followers of Jesus into the preacher, the confessor, and at last the martyr for Christ's sake.

In writing to the simple-minded people of Thessalonica, all this characteristic warmth of St. Paul's nature is called into activity. They were not a community of highly cultivated or courtly men and women, whose spiritual progress might be supposed to have had special attractiveness for the well-born Cilician Hebrew of the Hebrews, nurtured in the school of the philosophic Gamaliel. They were for the most part a hardy folk, of the old Macedonian type, gaining their living by the occupations belonging to a seaport town, while the higher families of the place felt the influence of the presence of the Roman governor of the province, whose official residence was fixed at Thessalonica and of the travellers along the great road leading to Byzantium.

V. As might be expected in the case of new converts in such a population, what they needed from their spiritual father was practical advice and consolation, rather than explanations of subtleties and bewildering speculations. Hence we find St. Paul assuming that they habitually recognized the practical value of prayer, as a means for obtaining the objects they desired from God. If they wanted him to visit them, they had only to pray for it, and he trusts that their prayers will be answered. Again and again phrases incidentally occur, showing how undoubting was the apostle's own faith in the efficacy of constant and earnest praying, and his certainty that the Thessalonians shared his faith. Of the fine-drawn distinctions between prayer for spiritual graces and prayer for temporal gifts, which now exercise so much influence on sincere Christians, these unsophisticated Thessalonians knew nothing. They had never heard of what we now call the laws of nature, and the molecular relations of the physical universe to its component parts. If they wanted rain, they prayed for it. If they wanted calm waters in the Ægean, they prayed that there might be calm; just as when they wanted a visit from St. Paul, they prayed for it.

Then, again, it is evident that they had not completely got rid of their old heathen habits of licentiousness and dishonest dealing, of which apparently some of them thought little.

But if there was one element in the practical life of the believers of Thessalonica which seems especially strange to most Christians of to-day, it was the manner in which they looked forward to a speedy termination of the existing constitution of the world, and the grounds on which they took comfort when grieving for the loss of those they loved. As was the case with all persons who were converted to the faith of Christ, their affections for one another were deepened by their newly learnt love of God. The mother learnt to mourn for her dead children, the sister for her brother, the husband for his wife, and the friend for the friend, with a sorrow that refused to be comforted by the fancies of pagan mythology, or even the faint hopes which the pious Jew gathered from the Old Testament Scriptures.

VI. To these wounded hearts St. Paul brought the Christian consolation. The resurrection of Jesus, he taught them, is the pledge of the resurrection of man, and of that reunion with those whom we have lost which alone can dry our tears. And to this reunion with the dead these Thessalonian Christians looked forward as about to occur under conditions the attractiveness of which many people to-day find it difficult to realize. The significant fact to be especially noted, when we recall the actual life of the Thessalonian Christians, is this—that they were not taught by St. Paul simply to look forward to a reunion with the dead in some future state of existence, but to expect it soon, through the reappearance of Christ Himself in this world. There is no doubt whatever as to the meaning of the apostle's teaching. The Lord will come, he said, and the dead in Christ will at once arise, and will be taken to meet the Lord, before us who are alive. He does not say, before those who will be alive. He speaks of himself and the faithful in Thessalonica as being still alive, and as being preceded by the risen dead to the immediate presence of Christ. Then the living and the dead would be united for ever. And in this expectation St. Paul bids the believers to find consolation in their sorrows for those whom they had loved and lost, and to comfort one another in their griefs.

That the believers took this consolation to heart, and that a conviction that Christ would speedily reappear entered deeply into their practical existence, is evident from St. Paul's second letter, and from the mischievous inferences which some of their number drew from the apostle's teaching. It was perhaps natural, in a hardworking race like the Thessalonians, to think that a freedom from laborious toil would be one of the chief delights of heaven; and it is not much to be wondered at that some of the more ignorant among them argued that if the present constitution of society was speedily to come to an end, they might as well anticipate the pleasures of a heavenly existence by taking at once to idleness, leaving to their wealthier neighbours the business of finding them food and such clothing as they needed. Probably they were somewhat surprised when St. Paul's second letter arrived, and they were told by him that those who would not work should be left to starve.

Accompanying this denunciation of selfish indolence, we find St. Paul implying that though he had written under a belief that he himself would be alive at the coming of Christ, he had uttered no word which might be regarded as a declaration that he really knew the precise period at which this coming might be looked for. In fact, it was impossible that he could ever have countenanced such a notion. Though he was not present on the occasion described in the beginning of the Acts of the Apostles, he must have been well aware that on that occasion the Lord had expressly declared that the knowledge of the dates of coming events was no part of the revelation which He commissioned the apostles to teach to all the nations of the earth.

At the same time, while St. Paul thus cautioned the Thessalonians against assuming that the Lord either was or was not about to return, he told them that this return must undoubtedly be preceded by a certain event which had not then taken place. This event was the completion of the anti-Christian and idolatrous work of a certain power whom he terms "the man of sin," whose machinations were already beginning when the letter was written. Who or what was this man of sin, and what was the controlling power that partially restrained these deadly results, no one now really knows. It is to be remarked, however, that St. Paul seems to expect that the people of Thessalonica would without difficulty understand his meaning, at least as a practical warning.

VII. And thus we are able to complete our picture of the daily life of the brave and faithful souls who fought the good fight more than eighteen centuries ago, and who were the first Christian community who enjoyed the privilege of receiving a letter signed by the hand of the great apostle of the Gentiles. Nothing in the existing city of Salonica remains to suggest to the traveller that he sees the very stones of the buildings on which the great apostle's eyes rested when he came to the old city, and on those three sabbath days proclaimed that the tragedy on Calvary was the murder of the incarnate Son of God. It is different in some other of those venerable sites, such as Corinth or Ephesus; and now at last there are fragments of the famous Ephesian temple of Diana to be seen in London itself. Yet the daily life of the Christians of Thessalonica can be recalled in all its completeness. An active, vigorous, and hearty race; not poetical, nor controversial, nor metaphysical, they received the gospel as a guide to their conduct and a consolation in their troubles. Their unbelieving Jewish neighbours might persecute, and their Gentile neighbours might jeer at them, but they went on believing in Jesus and His promises, and whatever they wanted they prayed for. They stood by the graves of those whom they had loved and lost, and wondered how soon those graves would open, and the living forms of the dead in Christ would rise, and meet Him as He came in His glory. In what way, they asked one another, was the mystery of iniquity, the man of sin, now working? Was it, perhaps, at their very doors? Who could say? And they asked one another all the more eagerly and anxiously when ships from various ports in the Mediterranean sailed into their harbour, and people who had been to Rome or Byzantium brought news of the growing audacities of the imperial soldiery, and the weakness and folly of the feeble-minded Claudius who now sat upon the throne once filled by the magnificent Augustus. What did it all portend to themselves? And why, they could not help asking, is the Lord so long in coming? What harm could there be in entreating Him to come quickly? When they repeated His own prayer again, and said, "Thy kingdom come," it was only natural that in their hearts they should mean, "May Thy visible kingdom come quickly."

Such was the Church of Thessalonica eighteen hundred and thirty years ago. Imperial Rome was in her decline, and hastening to her fall, though it was long delayed. Byzantium, the new Rome, of which these Thessalonians heard so much, soon to be transformed into Constantinople, was giving promise of its future splendours, with nothing to foreshadow the fate that awaited it, or of that last destiny which is still hidden from our modern eyes.

All now is changed. The Moslem, with his ruthless foot, has trampled upon the very spot where the saintly lips of the great apostle once proclaimed the unsearchable riches of Christ. All is changed and gone, except that faith and love which Divine grace infused into the souls of those devout believers, whose very names are unknown to us. That faith and love will still survive in every Christian heart till the purposes of God are accomplished; and then Jesus will be once more amongst us, not in His humiliation, but in His power and glory.

CHAPTER IV.

GALATIA.

I. A STRIKING illustration of the differences of character which marked the Christians of the apostolic age is supplied by the letter which St. Paul wrote to the Churches of Galatia shortly after he wrote his Second Epistle to the Thessalonians. Thessalonica was not far from the southern border of the province of Asia Minor, in those days called Galatia; but in reading the Epistle to the Galatians we seem to be passing into a new world of thought and feeling. The simplicity, the steadfastness, and the cordiality of the Thessalonians have all vanished, and the tone of the apostle's remonstrances to the Galatians bears little resemblance to that of the warm-hearted, thankful sentences in which he writes to the faithful men and women of Thessalonica. Of course he is still the same man himself, and the lovingness of his nature breaks out in the midst of the indignant remonstrances which he addresses to his unstable converts, both of Jewish and Gentile origin. Yet the general impression which the letter gives of the Galatian Christians is not agreeable.

And it is only by remembering the peculiar influences which Judaism exercised upon the Jews of the day that we can at all understand the state of mind of the Galatian believers. The controversies which agitated them have passed so completely into the regions of extinct speculations, that we study St. Paul's reasonings with a half-antiquarian interest, wondering at the angry character of the disputes which made Galatia the reverse of a home of peace and quiet. It is only by recollecting that the roots of the controversy lay deep in the unchangeable infirmities of human nature that we can recognize in much of the apostle's argument anything that practically concerns ourselves. From this point of view the condition of the Galatian Churches is full of interest, and abounds with suggestions of the utmost consequence.

II. Situated in the middle of Asia Minor, the district of Galatia was within an easy distance from Thessalonica. The peculiar origin of the population of Galatia partly accounts for the peculiarities of its people when converted to the faith of the gospel. A colony of the Gaulish invaders of the Roman Republic had settled in this part of Asia Minor, giving their name to the district, and had been mingled, rather than united, with the people of other races who inhabited the territory. In St. Paul's days the Gaulish temperament was as unchanged as it is to this day in France; and when it came into contact with Greek, or Asiatic, or, still more, with Jewish influences, it exhibited all the characteristics of an impulsive, though bold and energetic nature.

Thus it was, that while in Thessalonica the spirit of Judaism chiefly affected the unconverted Jews, whom it excited to personal violence towards Paul and Silas, in Galatia the mischief it worked was far more serious, as it affected the converted Jews themselves. The believers were thus divided into two parties; and if it can hardly be said that the two broke out into open hostility, their disputes were incessant, and the very springs of Christian love and good works were poisoned. The Jews, though sincerely converted, took the admission of the Gentiles to the privileges of the Gospel with a very ill grace. They had found it useless to contend not only against the reasonings of Paul, the avowed apostle of the Gentiles, but against the authority of Peter himself, who had been at one time inclined to the national exclusiveness, though he had yielded to the determined remonstrances and public opposition of Paul. But, having unwillingly submitted, they, or at least the leading men among them, adopted a new line of argument, at first sight so plausible, that, when urged with the characteristic persistency of their race, it bewildered the Gentile converts. Not being attached to St. Paul himself with the fervour of devotion and admiration of the warm-hearted Thessalonians, and not loving the self-denying precepts of the gospel with any very practical love, these Galatian Gentiles had little to fall back upon, when their Jewish fellow-converts gave them no peace, tormenting them with assertions that every Gentile Christian was bound to be circumcised, alleging that the law of Moses, being confessedly given by God, could not be abrogated, and was of universal obligation till the end of the world.

As they were unable to detect the fallacy which this theory embodied, the whole personal life of the Gentile converts was disturbed and materially suffered. How could it be otherwise? It was difficult enough for men who had been brought up in the self-indulgent, unloving habits of heathenism to master their passions, and adopt the law of Christ, surrounded as they were by fellow-countrymen devoted to jovialities and revellings, and as quarrelsome as they were licentious. And when to these trials of their morality were added the astounding assertions of their Jewish fellow-Christians, claiming to be more enlightened than themselves, their whole spiritual life was endangered, and their peace of mind was well-nigh gone.

III. What was the extent of the reform which was effected by St. Paul's letter to them we have no means of knowing. But it must have been thorough, for it attacked their errors at the very root. The letter is not long, but it states the whole case in St. Paul's most forcible manner. The law of Moses, he says, was undoubtedly of Divine origin, but it was designed to serve one special purpose; and when it had served that purpose, all its ceremonial enactments, including the observance of certain days and years as sacred, were abrogated. The one purpose of the Mosaic law was to teach man his utter helplessness when dependent upon himself; and thus, as a schoolmaster, to bring him to Christ. It bade man attempt a perfect life as a work within his own capacity, and with all the help that ceremonial observances could give him, and then to mark the result. Absolute failure was sure to follow, for in such a case nothing less than complete success in every detail could be accepted. If man was to stand upon his own rights before God, he could not present himself as half a sinner and half a saint. The bond was absolute in the conditions which it required to be fulfilled. To state the Jewish view was, in fact, to disprove it. Man, without a mediator, and without the indwelling of a Divine Spirit in his soul, cannot present himself with any claims before God. Thus he is compelled to have recourse to the mediation and help of Christ; and the law of Moses, having thus fulfilled its purpose, is abolished, except, of course, in those duties of morality which existed from the first moment of man's creation, and were not created by any positive enactments of Moses. These duties the grace of Christ now made it possible for man to fulfil in all their completeness. In the sight of God, therefore, the one question was, not what race or community a man belonged to, but whether or not his nature was renewed by the operation of the Holy Spirit of God.

IV. As for the conduct of the Galatians themselves, St. Paul tells them in the plainest terms that, while busying themselves with this miserable controversy, they had been neglecting the first duties of the moral law, enforced by the teaching of Christ, as they must have understood it from his own instructions when with them.

All this, in truth, gives a melancholy, though, perhaps, not very surprising picture of the spiritual condition of the Christians of these towns and villages scattered about this Asiatic province. What does surprise us is their treatment of St. Paul himself. This treatment is an illustration of the effect which clearness of aim and tenacity of purpose exercise in all human affairs. The non-Jewish inhabitants of Galatia being a mixed race, in whom the old Gaulish nature, itself impetuous rather than persevering, was not thoroughly welded with the Greek, Roman, and Asiatic elements into one homogeneous character, could not resist the dogged pertinacity of a people so intensely national and united as the children of Abraham have remained from generation to generation. Accordingly, when the Jewish party set to work to undermine St. Paul's apostolic authority, which was confessedly hostile to their pretensions, the wavering Gentile converts could not devise any sufficient reply. All through the Galatian district, what we should now call the *mot d'ordre* was given to the Jewish members of the Church; and whenever a Gentile pleaded St. Paul's authority against the intolerable pretensions of the Jewish partisans, Who is this Paul, it was asked, that we should submit ourselves to his dictation? He calls himself an apostle; but every one knows that while Jesus was alive, he hated those who believed in Jesus. The real apostles are all at Jerusalem. Has Peter authorized Paul to upset the law of Moses? Have any of those who are at Jerusalem sanctioned his teaching? Did he ever pretend that they had? He is nobody; and if you Gentiles wish to be saved you must submit to the laws of Moses, however much you may dislike them.

V. When Paul heard of this avowed rebellion against his authority, his indignation was unconcealed; and the Christian Church of all ages is under the deepest obligations to the perverse Galatians for having thus drawn from the great apostle of the Gentiles a statement in detail of the course of his personal history after his conversion. How much we thus owe to the fickleness of these people, and to the perverse ingenuity of the Jews among them, it is not easy to estimate. It was the same in their case as in that of other Churches, whose internal condition gave occasion to the writing of that wonderful series of letters which have become the treasure of the Church in all ages.

The Epistle to the Galatians, indeed, in a remarkable degree reminds us of the soundness of the principle recognized in the present inquiry, and convinces the Biblical student that then only can these Epistles be estimated at their correct value, and be rightly understood, when they are studied as actual letters called forth, in each case, by peculiar circumstances, and that it is absurd to read St. Paul's writings as if they were a collection of theological documents, published, as it were, by him for the benefit of believers in general. As we read this Epistle, we are continually called to remember that they are *bonâ fide* letters, written to actual persons, with especial reference to their circumstances and their conduct. Their style, again, is for the most part almost colloquial, and though it bears no trace of hastiness, yet the letters often pass from one subject to another without formal method or arrangement, just like other letters which are intended by their writers to be personal communications, and not essays put forth to the world under the guise of Epistles.

Thus it is that, when we study St. Paul's letter to these fickle Galatians, it is at first really difficult to understand the condition of a Christian society which called for such assertions of the writer's apostolic claims as we now read after the lapse of so many centuries. Still, these claims must have been to some extent new to the Galatian believers. When they vacillated between the true gospel and a mock reproduction of Judaism, they could hardly have been prepared to hear that St. Paul did not receive his apostolic commission from the original apostles, but supernaturally from Jesus Himself; and that the same Jesus who thus gave him his commission to preach the gospel, supernaturally communicated to him a knowledge of its doctrines. Thus, when the Galatians were instructed by their teacher in the faith of Christ, it was as if they were listening to the very words of the crucified and risen Redeemer; and no man, whether Jew or Gentile, could dare to gainsay His teaching.

What was the final impression produced upon the Galatian believers by St. Paul's letter we have no means of knowing. We can but speculate upon the discussions it aroused in the towns and villages scattered about on the mountainous slopes of the whole region. It is impossible to set a limit to the operations of Divine grace, and it may be that the Galatian Christians were so changed as to become saints and even martyrs for Christ. If they were thus changed, they would deserve to be recorded among the brightest examples of the power of the Holy Ghost, enlightening human stupidity and making the fairest flowers grow in the most uncongenial soils.

CHAPTER V.

CORINTH.

I. WHEN St. Paul had finished his work in Macedonia, he went on, with his companions, to Athens, on his way to Corinth. His visit to Athens was one of the most memorable of those which are described in the Acts of the Apostles, as it was there that he delivered the famous address, in which he explained the spiritual nature of the Godhead, and recognized the holiest motives of many of the heathen world in their efforts to penetrate into the mystery of the unseen. This visit to Athens has also a special interest for us who are of the English race, as we have in our possession the actual sculptures of the superb temple which was the glory of Athens and the envy of all Greece when St. Paul was there. When we stand before those wonderful marbles, our pulse throbs quicker and our eyes glisten, as we remember that when the great apostle of the Gentiles walked through the streets of Athens and watched the devotions of the people he had before him, those identical bas-reliefs which then adorned the frieze of the Parthenon, and which, now known as the Elgin Marbles, are among the most precious relics of antiquity that time has spared, to show us what Greek art was in the days of its glory. St. Paul, however, thought nothing of Phidias, or of that statue of ivory and gold within the temple in which the greatest of sculptors had embodied the highest conceptions of eternal wisdom to which the Greek intellect had attained; for his heart was stirred within him as he reflected that these men of Athens, with all their acuteness and philosophy, were so utterly ignorant of real wisdom that they worshipped their fabled goddess Minerva as their ideal and virgin teacher, and yet imagined that the essence of the Godhead was such that the Eternal One could live in temples made by human hands.

II. And then he saw an altar with a strange inscription, which awakened all his sympathetic pity, for it was addressed "to the unknown God." What would we not give now if, in addition to the bas-reliefs of the combats of the Centaurs and the Lapithæ, we could discover that identical altar, reared to the unknown divinity, by a people so much given * to worship the unseen powers, that their piety, ignorant as it was, called forth the apostle's ungrudging praises?

III. When, then, with the recollections of Athens still haunting his memory, St. Paul went on to Corinth, he found himself in another world. In

* Δεισιδαιμονεστεροι.

Athens the glory of the city was a temple reared in honour of wisdom. In Corinth they gloried in a temple raised to the goddess of carnal love; and what Minerva was to the Athenians, Venus was to the Corinthians, with whom the most unrestrained licentiousness was recognized as lawful and honourable.

And thus it came about that when the apostle, after founding a Christian Church in the heart of that city of pleasure, went on his journey, and shortly afterwards wrote his letters to the Corinthian believers, we find him again and again contrasting the wisdom of the Greeks with the true wisdom of the gospel. The influence of what he had seen and heard in Athens was evidently still powerful in his recollections; at the same time that both of the letters to the Corinthians show that a belief in the perfection of human philosophy was as dominant among them as among the less licentious and more speculative people of Athens. The practical difference between the religions of the two cities was indeed great. No altar dedicated to an unknown God was to be seen in Corinth. They cared only for the subtleties of the Greek philosophy, so far as its proud self-sufficiency left the enjoyments of life unrestrained by any stern or severe morality. Athens might cry out in her distress to the unseen and unknown. It was enough for Corinth that she had the Paphian goddess for her tutelary divinity.

St. Paul's two Epistles record, at the same time,

some singular aberrations of thought among the Corinthian converts. Many of them being of Jewish origin, the influence of the Jewish party in the whole community was considerable. In fact, Crispus, the chief person in the synagogue, had become a Christian; and from the salutation in the beginning of the first Epistle, which includes the name of Sosthenes, it appears that the gospel had been received by the very man who had instigated the mob of Jews in the city to drag Paul and Silas before Gallio, the Roman Governor of Corinth and of all Achaia.

IV. St. Paul's whole stay in Corinth lasted about eighteen months, and when at last he went away, he supposed that the believers were an enlightened community, and that neither the moral corruptness of the place nor the vain speculations of heathen philosophy would materially interfere with their spiritual progress. He was not a little surprised and disappointed. The spirit of sectarianism, which was a natural result of the division into opposing schools of thought among the Greek philosophers, gave birth to divisions among the Corinthian Christians which, to our modern judgment, appear as ludicrous as they were in reality serious. There was no specifically Jewish party in Corinth as there was in the more rustic population of Galatia. The divisions of the Corinthians were essentially Greek, a result of the national fondness for the dialectic methods of the philosophers ; only, instead of ranking themselves as Stoics, or Epicureans, or devotees of the Academy, they separated into petty sects, calling themselves by the names of their Christian instructors. Some of them declared that they followed the doctrine of Paul, others that of Apollos, others that of Cephas, and others that of Christ. A curious spectacle they must have presented to their heathen fellow-citizens, still satisfied with their own worship of Venus, and upholding her unholy rites. This result, of course, troubled the Corinthian sectarians but little, or not at all. Men and women who could persuade themselves that the gospel of the crucified Jesus was not essentially one, but might be modified at the will of the teachers who proclaimed it, were not likely to distress themselves about the disedifying effect of their quarrels upon their unbelieving neighbours. To us, who see in these Corinthian parties only a caricature of the partisanship of the disciples of Zeno and Epicurus and Aristotle, their essentially anti-Christian character is evident enough, and they seem almost childish in their shallowness.

To St. Paul, however, they seemed to demand the most serious refutation; and in the manner of the refutation which he wrote to them we cannot help recognizing the impression which had been made upon his feelings by all that he had lately been seeing at Athens. The whole community of Corinthian Christians was, in truth, agitated by these squabbles of a knot of self-satisfied schismatics, and

St. Paul treats their divisions as intimately connected with a certain error of vital moment, which more or less affected the faith of the entire Corinthian Church. With certain exceptions, they were all infected with that pride of the Greek philosophers which blinded them to the perception of the truth which lies at the root of the gospel system; the truth, that is, that suffering is, by the ordinance of God, appointed to be the instrument for the redemption of humanity from all the evils that afflict it. This is the law of the cross; and it was this law which appeared simply ridiculous in the eyes of the Greek teachers of wisdom. The various philosophic sects had each of them their peculiar methods of reasoning, and they set up different standards of perfection to be aimed at by the chosen few who could rise above the level of the vulgar herd. But in all their speculations they never penetrated to the heart of the great mystery which enshrouds the destiny of our race, or solved the one inscrutable problem.

V. From their hereditary national belief in the value of these various philosophic theories, the Christians of Corinth had by no means freed themselves. The fundamental law of the gospel, that every good thing comes to the soul of man through suffering, was still very imperfectly grasped by them. And yet, as St. Paul reminds them, the proofs of the helplessness of human wisdom were constantly before their eyes. The followers of the crucified

Jesus were, indeed, multiplying in Corinth and elsewhere, but for the most part they were of the plebeian and uncultivated classes; not noble, or wealthy, or learned; but shopkeepers, like Lydia of Thyatira, who sold scarlet silk and cloth; or tent-makers, like Aquila and Priscilla.

What could the philosophers make of such a religion as this? The fables of heathen mythology they taught were of course false; but there was something grand and beautiful about many of them. It was impossible to laugh at the idea of the cloud-compelling Jove, or of Pallas, the goddess of wisdom, worshipped with so much splendour by the people of Athens. And as for their own favourite goddess of pleasure, the devotion of Corinth to her rites might be excessive, but nevertheless their Venus was the embodiment of all that is lovely in humanity.

As for this new God of the Christians, what cultivated intellect could admit His claims? He was a Jew, which fact alone was enough to predispose the lordly Greek mind to ridicule Him. And He was a poor man, and His mother, though of royal ancestry, was an obscure person. He was treated by the Jews themselves as a malefactor, and put to a shameful death. Who could regard as anything but foolish a doctrine which taught that this crucifixion was the source of human redemption?

So argued the philosophers of Corinth, and with so much success that not a few of the new converts were bewildered, and failed to cling to the truth which excited the scorn of the Greek thinkers, as the very essence of the gospel which they had learnt from the apostle of Jesus himself.

As a consequence of this inadequate conception of the gospel as a law of suffering and death, they were staggered by the objections which they heard made to the doctrine of the resurrection of the body. The argument in which St. Paul points out the philosophic flaw in the difficulty felt by the Corinthian Christians is a signal illustration both of the wide range of his own philosophic thought and of the beauty and force of rhetorical style to which he could rise when his subject demanded it. Taken in connection with the exposition of the nature of Christian charity in the same Epistle, this famous passage shows that the great apostle's powers as a writer were on a level with those of the greatest masters, both in poetry and prose; and we cannot doubt that, as a speaker, he rivalled the most renowned orators of Greece and Rome.

VI. The difficulty which distressed the minds of the Corinthian Christians was, indeed, plausible, and required a carefully reasoned answer. How *can* there be such a thing as a resurrection of these miserable bodies of ours? The very conception of such a futurity brings its own refutation with it. Thus they argued, and could see no way out of the difficulty. St. Paul's reply is complete. Your difficulty, he says, shows that you have not learnt the obvious lesson which is taught by our gardens and fields and by the skies above us. The whole animal and vegetable world exhibits endless varieties of species, serving many different purposes, and all alike the work of the Almighty Creator's hand. To limit our conceptions of the essential nature of the human body to our experience of its present capacities is to overlook all the facts of physical science, involving a violation of all the laws of reasoning. We cannot assume that there is only one possible type of corporeal framework for our non-corporeal souls, for the universe abounds with innumerable varieties in every part.

But, further, the law of decay and reproduction from that which decays is universal with our plants and trees. The seed falls into the ground and seems to perish, but it carries within it the germ of a new life, which is practically brought about by its own dissolution into the dust of the earth. When, then, he concludes, I teach you the doctrine which I have learnt from the risen and glorified Jesus, I teach you nothing to which a sound philosophy can make any objection.

VII. The Corinthian Church was, in fact, one of the most intellectually gifted of all the apostolic Churches. And, with all the foolish sectarian divisions which disturbed them, they were personally a noble example of the power of the gospel in moulding men's lives in the midst of one of the most sceptical and licentious centres of Greek heathenism. They had a character of their own, unlike that of the good, simple-hearted Thessalonians or the more rustic inhabitants of the villages clustered on the hilly slopes of Galatia. Indeed, it is impossible to imagine St. Paul sending either to Thessalonica or Galatia such letters as he addressed to the more subtle intellects of Corinth. The very character of the faults against which he remonstrates in writing to the Corinthians, his method of appealing to their cultivated intelligence, prove the profound interest with which they had inspired him. To them, if not with all the hearty fulness with which he wrote to his beloved flock at Thessalonica, yet with most spontaneous cordiality, he poured forth all that sweet tenderness of feeling which was his most winning characteristic.

VIII. To us, after the lapse of so many centuries, and living in a state of society and civilization which would have roused the wonder and, in some respects, the ridicule of Corinth and Athens, the social and personal life of the Corinthian Christians is still a subject which awakens keen curiosity and suggests anxious reflections. First of all, the strictly miraculous powers* sometimes conferred upon His servants by the Divine Head of the Church were evidently by no means uncommon in Corinth. What St. Paul writes leaves no room for doubt in the matter. Some of them could heal diseases; some could speak in languages which they had never learnt, not always themselves under-

* See chap. xxi.

standing the meaning of the words they uttered; others could interpret the meaning of the words thus uttered by those who possessed the gift of tongues. But whatever are the precise ideas which we are to attach to these expressions of the apostle, it is undeniable that the Corinthians were familiar with the practical exercise of powers of an unquestionably miraculous kind, and that the possession of these gifts, as an effect of the presence of the Holy Ghost in the soul, was not regarded by St. Paul as an altogether exceptional phenomenon.

IX. We must take it for granted, then, that for some special reason, unknown to us, it was the will of God that in this city of sensuality, frivolity, and intellectual conceit the heathen inhabitants should see in the midst of them a certain community of men and women, for the most part not belonging to the higher classes of society, counting among its members persons who could heal the sick, or declare truths unknown to man, or speak languages which they had not learnt by the ordinary methods of learning. All this, too, they asserted to be the effect of the presence of a Divine *afflatus*, communicated to them by the crucified Son of a Jewish virgin mother, who had risen from the dead, and was now administering the affairs of His followers, though Himself unseen. What a marvellous spectacle! And not less marvellous was the fact that, with whatever occasional failings, these people repudiated the old sensual, passionate life of heathenism, and devoted themselves to a life of purity, humility, and the patient love of their fellow-creatures.

One strange abuse, which had crept in among the Corinthian Christians, was no doubt unknown to their heathen neighbours, as it was confined to their private assemblies, when they met to celebrate the Lord's Supper. The passage in the Epistle in which St. Paul denounces this abuse is not easy to understand in all its expressions, but its general bearing is clear enough. The habitual practice of the believers brought into prominence the fact that, even on such an occasion as this, the distinction between the rich and the poor was not kept out of sight. The poor came to celebrate the Last Supper with keen appetites, which they took the opportunity of then satisfying, eating and drinking to supply the wants which they could not satisfy in their own houses. The behaviour of the wealthy appears to have been more decorous, though St. Paul censures them severely for putting the poor to shame. The censure, in fact, was addressed to the Corinthians as a community. Its chief value to ourselves consists in the account which it led St. Paul to give of the actual institution of the Lord's Supper, as made known to him by the special revelation of Jesus Christ, and not derived from information which he had gathered from the other apostles.

Taking the Epistle, then, as a whole, it is not surprising that when St. Paul wrote a second time to the Corinthian believers, the tone of his letter is a good deal changed. Once more the extraordinary sweetness of his nature inspires him to enter upon details in his personal history, such as a man writes only to those whom he loves; though he has still to rebuke the Corinthians for some of their old faults. He tells them of the extraordinary favours bestowed by the Divine goodness upon himself; how it pleased God to afflict him with "a thorn in the flesh," in order to keep him humble; and how, when he prayed earnestly for its removal, the Lord had bidden him to bear it patiently, strengthened by the power of that grace whose aid is most conspicuous when human frailty is weakest. Then, further, he reminds them of all his own labours and sufferings in the cause of the gospel, a catalogue little short of appalling to ordinary men, and proving that, besides all his other personal qualifications, the great apostle possessed a physical constitution and extraordinary powers of endurance.

Altogether, we are impressed with a confidence that the daily life of the Corinthian Christians became a striking illustration of the power of that preaching of the cross which has convinced men in every age that death is the source of all life, and suffering the source of all joy and peace.

CHAPTER VI.

ROME.

I. THE precise year in which the Epistle to the Romans was written is not known with such accuracy as to place it beyond dispute. But for our present purpose it may be taken for granted that it was written soon after the Epistles to the Corinthians. It certainly was written after the first of the two.

St. Paul's visit to Rome is recorded in the concluding chapter of the Acts of the Apostles, which ends with the statement that he passed two years there, living in a house which he rented for himself, preaching the gospel without hindrance to every one who came to hear him.

His position in Rome was singular, and strikingly illustrates the real attitude of the Roman authorities towards the first preachers of the gospel, and the toleration, mingled with a certain contempt, which the mighty rulers of the world accorded to the religion of the crucified Jesus. This tolerant spirit was characteristic of the practical and haughty Roman intellect. It was the guiding influence in the mind of Pontius Pilate himself; and it must be remembered that it was the Roman governor of the province of Achaia who would have nothing to do with the charges brought against the great apostle by the fiery Jews of Corinth. And now that he had come to Rome, in consequence of his appeal as a freeborn Roman citizen to the imperial tribunal, he was controlled as little as was possible in the case of a person charged with treason by his own fellow-countrymen. He was placed under the guardianship of a private soldier, who lived in the house with him, and who doubtless troubled himself little enough with the doings of one whom he regarded with some wonder, though probably with much personal regard.

We have no information in the Acts of the Apostles respecting the first preaching of the gospel in Rome. It seems most likely that the first converts came from Jerusalem, after the miraculous descent of the Holy Ghost on the day of Pentecost, as recorded in the second chapter of the Acts. It is expressly stated that among the believers then present were strangers from Rome, both of the original Hebrew race and of the class known as proselytes. These men must have returned to Rome, after sharing in the gifts conferred by the great miracle, and must have communicated to their friends the wonders they had seen and heard. And thus the foundation of a Church was laid, and a preparation made for the instructions which St.

Paul would give, when his appeal to Cæsar brought him nominally, but scarcely in reality, a prisoner to the imperial city.

And this belief as to the origin of the Roman Church is confirmed by the character which St. Paul found prevailing among the Roman Christians when he at length reached the imperial city. They were intensely Jewish in their habits of thought, and practically resisted the calling of the Gentiles to the utmost of their power, confirming the apostle's general experience of the serious obstacle which the Judaism of the day presented to the progress of the gospel. Heathenism had its own characteristic sins to answer for, but the sins of Judaism were still more obstinate in hardening men's minds against a creed which struck at pride as the most deadly of all moral evils.

From the letter, however, which St. Paul afterwards wrote to the Romans, it is evident that this spirit of proud independence had infected the Roman Christians generally, though the Jewish members of the Church were worse than the converted Gentiles.

II. This, indeed, was what might have been expected in the inhabitants of the imperial city, the Christians as a rule glorying in their title to be regarded as Roman citizens. Rome was the metropolis of power, as Athens was the metropolis of the intellect, and Corinth the metropolis of pleasure. She was mistress of all the known world.

Her armies subdued every people that resisted her; and if she herself was no longer a free republic, the master to whom she had bowed her neck was, after all, the first of Roman citizens, and it was more glorious to be the subject of a Cæsar than to be the inhabitant of any free republic on the face of the earth.

III. In the recognition of this characteristic haughtiness we have a key to the understanding of the general drift of the Epistle to the Romans. With the exception of the numerous salutations to individuals in the last chapter, it contains few of those personal details which appear in the Epistles to the Thessalonians and the Corinthians, and from first to last seems to be devoted to the working out of the great truth, that God is supreme over all things that exist; that with Him there is no respect of persons; that the pride and self-sufficiency of the Jew were odious in His sight, and that there is only one way of salvation alike for Jew and Gentile, that is, the way of faith; in other words, the seeking for it as a free gift at the hands of God. The whole argument culminates in the celebrated passage in the eighth chapter, in which the apostle expounds in detail the doctrine of the eternal foreknowledge of God, and of the predestination of the elect. This predestination, he also points out, includes a predestination to a life of personal holiness according to the Christian standard, thus condemning every one who might abuse the doctrine of predestination as excusing indulgence in sin.*

Following up this exposition, he introduces the illustration of the potter and his clay, out of which the potter fashions one vessel to noble and beautiful purposes, and another for useful but inglorious services, in every case solely according to his own will.

Throughout the whole letter this is the truth which St. Paul impresses upon the haughty, domineering Roman mind; a truth, it is obvious to remark, not a little applicable to the typical Englishman of to-day, who glories in being the modern representative of the mighty Roman of the past, and dislikes to be reminded that, if he differs from other races, it is the sovereign and predestinating will of God which alone has made him what he is.

IV. As for the Roman Church itself, what makes its internal life especially attractive to us is the long list of devout men and women to whom St. Paul sends his affectionate greetings. They were a holy community, whatever their national faults, and St. Paul refers to their widely spread reputation in the beginning of the Epistle. But the reality of their devout spirit and of their love for one another is brought out in the clearest light by this mention of the many pious people of different classes to whom St. Paul sends his greetings. He is still the same Paul as of old; fierce and passionate as a

* See chap. xx.

persecutor before he understood what the gospel really was, but now overflowing with unaffected friendliness to every one whom he knew. In all his Epistles there are few things more touching than this long list of persons never forgotten by that heroic heart; heroic in its sweetness as well as in its strength, and before very long to beat with its last throb, dying for the crucified Jesus, among his much-loved saints in Rome.

V. Three years after his first visit he returned, never more to leave Rome alive. The interval was spent in carrying on his apostolic labours, and when he came back, he foresaw that the Master whom he served would soon take him to his reward. Nero, the bloodthirsty persecutor of the Christians, held the imperial sceptre, abhorred as he was; and in A.D. 66 the great apostle was taken from the Mamertine prison, into which he had been thrown, and beheaded.

That prison still remains; and surely, of all things that are to be seen in Rome, it awakens the sweetest and saddest memories. The splendours of Christian art, the very church that was built over the spot where tradition says that St. Paul was buried, the catacombs themselves, hardly touch our hearts as we are touched by the sight of the walls of that gloomy cell where the martyr awaited in peace the executioner's sword. That the blow was indeed welcome we cannot doubt. He had told his friends that though he was willing to live for the good of others, yet he had a desire to depart and to be with Christ. Who can wonder that at last even that resolute heart was weary? He had long ago renounced his own will; and if he rejoiced in being at last set free, it was still because he knew that it was the will of his risen Lord that His servant should now come to see Him in His glory.

CHAPTER VII.

EPHESUS.

I. THE Epistle to the Ephesians, which was written about A.D. 61, is one of those which forcibly illustrate the many varieties of type that existed among the Churches of the apostolic period. It differs from the letters which up to this time had been written by St. Paul, in being mainly devoted to the development of contemplative theology of the mystical kind.

The account of St. Paul's visit to Ephesus, given in the Acts of the Apostles, details some of the most surprising incidents which befell him in the whole course of his journeys before he reached Rome. The nucleus of the Ephesian Church was already in existence, though it numbered only about twelve members; all, apparently, of Jewish extraction. They knew little of the doctrines of the gospel, having been baptized with what was known as the baptism of John, which symbolized repentance from sin, and was simply a preparation for that baptism which conveyed the special Christian gift of the Holy Ghost to the penitent soul. Of this gift, indeed, they knew nothing; but when St. Paul baptized them with the baptism of Christ, they were at once filled with that Divine presence which makes all Christians the temple of the living God. Some of them, moreover, were put in possession of those miraculous powers which were given to the believers at Jerusalem on the day of Pentecost. Miracles, also, were wrought in connection with the person of the apostle himself, and altogether Ephesus was in a striking degree the scene of those marvellous manifestations of Divine power with which it pleased God at times to accompany the preaching of the truth.

II. From this time the gospel began to make its way, not only among the Jews and Gentiles of Ephesus, but throughout the whole of Asia Minor, of which Ephesus was one of the chief cities, holding a conspicuous place in the Ionic confederation, glorying in its wealth, and in the magnificence with which it worshipped the heathen goddess Diana. The temple of Diana was, in fact, one of the most superb in all Asia and Greece, though less perfect as a model of architectural beauty than the Athenian Parthenon; as Diana, the virgin daughter of Latona, was the embodiment of a less noble idea than that of the wisdom symbolized in the idea of the Athenian Minerva.

In promoting this worship of their favourite goddess the Ephesians spent their money lavishly, and supplied occupation to a numerous body of workers in silver. The success of St. Paul's preaching made these men furious; and one of their craft, by name Demetrius, stirred up a riot, which would have ended fatally for the apostle had he ventured into the infuriated mob. His friends, however, kept him concealed until the chief magistrate had, with great difficulty, quieted the rioters, when he left the city, and proceeded on his way to Macedonia.

III. Such were the circumstances under which the Christian faith was planted in Ephesus the magnificent. What was the condition of the famous city at the beginning of the present century modern travellers have informed us, with an instructive fulness of detail.

"On entering Ephesus," we are told, "the first objects seen are the remains of the *stadium*, or circus, the area of which is six hundred and eighty-seven feet in length, the northern or lower side having been raised on vaults, which still remain, the upper end resting on the slope of the hill. The seats have all been removed; and of the front only a few marbles and an arch remain. The area is a cornfield. The vestiges of a theatre are to be seen further on, in the side of the same mountain. The seats and the ruins of the front have been removed, but some architectural fragments and an inscription prove that this was the site of the theatre, probably that into which the mob rushed tumultuously at the instigation of Demetrius, crying, 'Great is Diana of the Ephesians!' Advancing from the theatre, we come to a narrow valley. Here are the ruins of a church, and vestiges of an *odeon*, or music-hall, and further still, the remains of a large structure resembling another at Troas, with an arcade. The top of one of the arches is painted with waves and fishes. This was the gymnasium, and was at the back of the city. Opposite to the stadium there remains a basin of white marble, streaked with red, about fifteen feet in diameter, and, according to Pococke, of a single stone. It is supposed to have belonged to a fountain, but one learned traveller thinks it was used for sacrifices, though there is a tradition that St. John baptized in it. Other ruins extend in the same direction, as the portico adjoining the theatre, having behind them a morass, once the city port. Near the highest of them, says Dr. Chandler, is the entrance of a subterraneous passage. Opposite to the portico is a vacant quadrangular space, with many bases of columns and marble fragments scattered about. Here it is probable was the *agora*, or market-place.

"The other remains are perhaps those of the arsenal, the public treasury, the prison, and the like buildings, which in the Greek cities were usually near the market-place. At the end of the street, and near the entrance of the valley, is the prostrate heap of a temple, the length four hundred and thirty feet, the breadth eighty feet. The *cella*, or nave, was constructed of large coarse stones. The portico was of marble, of the Corinthian order, the columns four feet six inches in diameter, and their height, including the base and the capital, more than forty-six feet. The shafts were fluted, and, though their dimensions were so great, each was cut from a single stone.

"But what," asks the same traveller, "has become of the temple of Diana? Can a wonder of the world have vanished like a phantom, without leaving a trace behind?" Then he expresses his regret at having searched for the site to as little purpose as preceding travellers, though its stones are known to have been far more ponderous than those of the columns above mentioned, and the size of the building larger beyond comparison than that of the ruined temple which remains. An ancient author has described it as standing at the head of the port, and shining like a meteor. Like a meteor it had disappeared. Later researches, however, have discovered portions of the Temple of Diana, and have proved that the size of its columns was quite as great as tradition had reported.

IV. Such has been the doom of the famous glories of that pagan worship, whose votaries attacked the apostle when he exposed the follies of idolatry. All this, too, must be carefully borne in mind while we examine the letter in which St. Paul taught the Christian Ephesians what are the mysteries of that spiritual religion which recognizes the true nature of the one Eternal God and of His presence in the soul of man.

In this examination into the subjects which St. Paul considered to be especially suitable to the character of the Ephesian believers, we have to bear in mind those peculiar manifestations of His power which God had displayed in the city where Diana was worshipped. The pagan Ephesians adored a certain imaginary being, and cherished as precious an image which they fancied had come down from Jupiter. To the chosen few who had learnt to reject these dreams, and to look to the crucified Jesus for enlightenment and help, God showed the effects of the presence of His Spirit in the soul, not only in its power of transforming the old helpless, sinful nature of man into a practical reflection of the Divine holiness, but in its conferring a visible power over the ordinary laws of the physical universe. By these supernatural phenomena the contrast between a faith in the one invisible God and a belief in the idols of Greek mythology was placed in the clearest light. The Christians in the city of Diana were enabled to comprehend with an intense vividness the reality of that spiritual presence in the believer's soul, which made him, to use the metaphor occasionally employed by St. Paul, the temple of the Holy Ghost.

V. Bearing all this in mind, we see the appropriateness of the peculiar subjects treated of by St. Paul in the Epistle to the Ephesians. He naturally begins his instructions with a brief exposition of the doctrine of predestination. From all eternity, he reminds the believers, God has foreseen and fore-ordained all things. This is the only possible explanation of the mystery of human life. As on other occasions, St. Paul does not here attempt to lead the human intellect into speculations which are beyond the reach of all created beings. He takes the simple fact, that there *is* an election of individual men and women to privileges which are denied to others. Then he points out what are the special privileges of Christians, what consequences those privileges involve, how they may be properly employed, and the moral obligations which accompany them. The whole Epistle is, in fact, a working out of the truths briefly summed up in the third chapter, when St. Paul says that he prays God that the Ephesians, being rooted and grounded in love, may be able to comprehend with all saints what is the breadth, and length, and depth, and height, and may know the love of Christ, which passes knowledge, and be filled with all the fulness of God. The whole work of God in Christ, he teaches, is a vast and profound mystery, which no created intelligence can thoroughly comprehend, but which is in a measure to be understood by those who approach the study of it with hearts filled with love. For love alone can understand love, and none but those who love the Lord Jesus in sincerity can hope to penetrate into the secrets of that Divine love which manifested itself in the incarnation of the Eternal Son in the womb of a virgin mother. To these favoured ones, seeking, in the midst of the distractions of this life, to know more of the hidden mystery, by the process, not of argument, but of contemplation, Jesus reveals Himself by the action of the Holy Spirit upon the heart and intellect already enlightened by the indwelling of that same Spirit. This is the essence of the mystical or contemplative life, to which all Christians are called, but which few attempt to attain in their own case. This is the main idea of St. Bernard's hymn, "Jesu, dulcis memoria;"* and of the "Imitatio Christi," in which À Kempis teaches that the action of the Holy Spirit upon the soul is *sine strepitu verborum;* without the sound or noise of human language.

Such, then, were the persons who, beneath the very shadow of Diana's temple, had learnt that wisdom which none of the princes of this world knew, and which, in the eyes of the haughty Jew and the subtle Greek alike, was a stumbling-block or mere foolishness. To us moderns it is, perhaps, as difficult to conceive ourselves in the midst of a state of society like that which thus existed among the Ephesian Christians as into that of Galatia or Corinth. We cannot, however, doubt that St. Paul well understood their intelligence and general spiritual condition, and we may constantly turn with delight to the thought of the course of their lives, and of the peaceful faith with which they meditated on the hidden mysteries

---

* "The love of Jesus, what it is,
None but His loved ones know."

of Divine love, and learnt to understand more and more fully the relations of the Eternal God towards the creatures of His will.

VI. We can imagine, too, what the superb city was in the days of its splendour, and see it on some festive day, when the prostrate and marble sculptures are reared again, and the great temple is hung with garlands, and the country people are flocking in from the neighbourhood to join in the merry-making and the religious ceremonial, and to catch a sight of the celebrated statue which they had been assured was sent down by Jupiter, king of gods and men, to represent his daughter Diana, the sister of Apollo, the great sun-god.

Then, from within and without the temple, shouts arise and fill the air. "Great is Diana of the Ephesians!" they cry, and toss up their arms into the air. Clouds of incense float around and intoxicate the senses, while the figures of richly-robed priests and priestesses lend solemnity to the dazzling scene. If Diana herself had appeared, visibly descending from the clouds, it would scarcely have astonished her devotees.

Meanwhile, here and there in the deserted streets of the city, or sitting in the now quiet stadium, a few men and women remain unmoved by the clamour. An inward voice is speaking to them without the sound of words. With their eyes they see only one Figure—the Figure of a Man with outstretched arms, fastened to a cross; and on His head is a crown, not of gold, but of thorns. As they look, their eyes half blinded with tears, the crucified Figure seems to fade away, and in its place is One seated on a royal throne, with a look of infinite tenderness upon His features. It is the same Jesus as before, now living to save and comfort His own loved ones, as only One who is God as well as man can save and comfort those for whom He has died. Thus, with the eyes of faith beholding the risen Jesus in His glory, their ears are deaf to the shouts of the excited crowds crying, "Great is Diana of the Ephesians!" Their ears, quickened by faith, hear only the hymn of the adoring multitudes before the throne, as with one voice they sing, "Alleluia! for the Lord God Omnipotent reigneth!" From star to star, and beyond every star in the firmament, in ineffably sweet harmonious modulations, men's, women's, and children's voices uniting in the marvellous chorus, the same song is echoed, and dies away and rises again in ever-varying notes of rapture—ever varying, but ever repeating the same strain, "Alleluia! for the Lord God Omnipotent reigneth!"

Such were the meditations of the devout people to whom the great apostle wrote this wonderful Epistle. And are they not still the meditations of those to whom it is given to listen to that inward voice, which, without the sound of words, unfolds more and more of the mystery that is hidden in the words, "Behold the Lamb of God, that taketh away the sin of the world"?

CHAPTER VIII.

COLOSSE.

I. THE Epistle to the Colossians was written from Rome about A.D. 62. In one respect it is perhaps of less interest than the Epistle to the Ephesians, which bears the manifest impress of the circumstances under which St. Paul preached the gospel at Ephesus. The Epistle to the Colossians does not suggest any recollections of the circumstances under which a Christian Church was founded at Colosse; but it supplies some striking illustrations of those peculiarities of thought and feeling which were characteristic of the apostolic period, and which find so few parallels in our modern times.

It especially illustrates the astonishing practical influence of the perverse Judaism of the day. Few people now realize the exact nature of this Judaism, or the extent to which it obstructed the progress of the pure spiritual Christianity of which St. Paul was the chief expounder. It is commonly imagined that when the prejudices of St. Peter were overcome by the vision described in the Acts of the Apostles, and the leader of the advocates of exclusiveness was thus himself converted, the way was made clear for the advance of the true gospel without let or hindrance.

The supposition is most erroneous. A knowledge of human nature, and especially of the old Jewish human nature, prepares us for the fact that exclusiveness and oligarchical haughtiness never died harder than they did when their aim was to shut out the enormous majority of the human race from the blessings of the salvation obtained by the sacrifice of the Son of God upon the cross.

II. Foiled in their desires to retain for themselves alone the privileges of the promised redemption, the disappointed Jews adopted a new device for ensuring for themselves a kind of hereditary supremacy in the newly created Church, from which they could not banish all Gentile intruders. The device was astute enough for the times, as the issue proved—easy as it is for us to detect its fallacy under the guidance of St. Paul's acute and penetrating exposure. Nothing is to us more evident than the essential distinction between the moral and the ceremonial portions of the law of Moses. Not so with the Christians of the apostolic age. From some cause, not at first sight very evident, they were often unable to perceive the distinction so obvious to ourselves; and their minds were thus open to the influence of those Judaizing notions which were the bane of so many of the local Churches.

To understand how this strange state of things came about it is necessary to examine carefully into the facts of the time, in order, if possible, to trace the popular currents of thought to their source, and so account for a condition of feeling otherwise inexplicable.

III. The explanation is to be found in that defective conception of the nature of the gospel itself which St. Paul's Epistles show to have prevailed to a serious extent among the first Christians. Human nature is human nature always and everywhere, even when men have learnt to accept the Son of Man as their Redeemer; and what human nature most desires is freedom from punishment for guilt.

Hence, while the believers rejoiced in the knowledge that by the sacrifice on the cross Jesus had reconciled them to an offended Judge, they paid comparatively little heed to what they were taught as to the main object of the Divine Sacrifice, namely, the transformation of their whole souls into a likeness to their Redeemer, through the action of an indwelling Spirit upon their hearts and lives. This, I say, was the result of the fact that they were human beings, loving ease and enjoyment, and valuing sanctity as a beautiful idea rather than as a personal reality.

On this account it was that St. Paul found it necessary to insist again and again upon the same truth, contemplating it from every point of view, illustrating it by various metaphors, and pointing out its connection with all the details of daily life, but always implying that this renewal of our whole nature by the gift of the Holy Ghost is the one transcendent object which God had in view when He gave His Son to die for our sins. In the eighth chapter of the Epistle to the Romans St. Paul condenses his constant teaching into one pregnant sentence. "What the law could not do," he says, "in that it was weak through the flesh, God sending His own Son in the likeness of sinful flesh, and as an offering for sin, condemned sin in the flesh, that the demands of the law might be fulfilled in us, who walk not after the flesh, but after the Spirit."

And it was from their faint perception of this great doctrine that the believers too often attained only an indistinct perception of the real nature of the new spiritual life in its essence and its details. They did not completely shake off the old pagan notion of virtue as a succession of formalities or ideas external to man's inner nature, and to be accomplished by his own self-reliant power. Of morality as residing in the heart, and of love as its essence, they had scarcely a glimmering conception.

IV. In the state of mind thus briefly described, the Gentile converts naturally did not take the alarm when their Jewish friends urged on them the necessity of accepting the law of Moses as a complete whole, without repudiating even its most arbitrary ceremonial regulations. One portion of this law seemed to them much the same as another, both in essential quality and in Divine sanction. They were, therefore, simply bewildered by the demands made upon them. When the Hebrew converts came and said to them, You must be circumcised ; you must not touch this thing or eat that ; you must observe certain days and months and years as holy; the unhappy men had not a word to say. If what their Jewish friends said was untrue, where was the authority of the ten commandments ? Did not the obligation to avoid murder and adultery rest on the same authority as the rite of circumcision ? If God commanded the one duty He also commanded the other. And thus in so many of the apostolic Churches the Judaizing party had their own way, at least to an extent which destroyed the harmony of the daily life of the believers.

V. At Colosse, which was itself an unimportant town in Phrygia, the influence of the Jewish pretensions seems to have been peculiarly disastrous. From many parts of the letter which St. Paul sent to them it is evident that not a few of their number were persons of great sanctity, and well deserved the name of saints with which he addressed them.

Nevertheless, the community as a whole did not see its way to the detection of the fallacies involved in the Judaizing theory, and it yields a most suggestive illustration of the singular conditions of the religious life of the time. The full details as to a Christian's duties which the Epistle contains suggest also a doubt as to whether the Judaizing speculations had not injuriously affected the general personal and domestic life of the believers. The instructions given by St. Paul seem so little to require enforcement, that we may conclude that there must have been something very faulty in a small community which could require guidance in such very obvious duties.

All experience, however, shows that any such conclusion would be superficial and rash. One must be both very conceited and very unobservant of the daily life of other people if one imagines that there is any relation between man and man in which the most conscientious minds are not liable to all sorts of self-deception, and do not require frequent self-examination in just such matters as those in which St. Paul instructs the Colossians. There is no reason for doubting that, if not furnishing an especially striking example of primitive saintliness, the Colossians were nevertheless a society of men and women whose lives were in marked contrast to the lives of the other Phrygian towns where the old heathenism had its way undisturbed. When the country was ravaged by an earthquake a few years later, and Colosse with many other places was destroyed, every reader of this Epistle must be satisfied that its Christian inhabitants were at all times ready for whatever fate might befall them. They were not faultless; but we cannot doubt that they died as they had lived, sincere and courageous Christians.

CHAPTER IX.

PHILIPPI.

I. THE very name of Philippi recalls associations contrasting with every Christian idea, yet reminding us of the great fact that the time was at length come when the promised Redeemer was to be born. The Roman empire was about to be consolidated into one united whole; and when man saw only the ruin of Republican armies before the hosts of the Imperialist factions, the foundations were laid for that despotic uniformity of administration which, with all its evils, made it possible for St. Paul and his companions to travel wherever they would, and carry the news of the gospel to all parts of the civilized world.

It was at Philippi that the great conflict was fought which issued in the deaths of Brutus and Cassius, and which before long made Octavius Cæsar master of every country that owned the Roman sway. It was in anticipation, too, of his coming fate at Philippi that an event occurred to Brutus himself, according to the story told by

Plutarch, which strikingly illustrates the practical side of that heathen philosophy which was about to enter upon a mortal struggle with the gospel, as one of its deadliest enemies.

The story is sufficiently curious to deserve repeating, simply in connection with the personal history of a man imbued with that very form of Greek philosophy which at first sight seems to be akin to the self-denying morality of the gospel. According to Plutarch, Brutus was one night sitting in his tent in the Republican camp, while the army was resting for a few hours on its way to meet the enemy, when, lifting up his eyes, he saw before him a terrible spectre. "Who art thou?" he asked, but little moved. "I am thine evil genius," replied the spectre, "and I will see thee again at Philippi." "I will meet thee there," replied Brutus; and the spectre disappeared. When Brutus told his friend Cassius what he had seen, Cassius laughed at him, and declared his conviction that the whole thing was an illusion, produced by bodily derangement, the consequence of fatigue and want of sleep. Cassius held the opinions taught by the philosopher Epicurus, who asserted that there are no such beings as spectres or demons, or that, if there are, they take no part in human affairs. Brutus, on the contrary, was a follower of Zeno and the Stoical philosophy, whose stern morality bore a certain resemblance to the proud Judaism of the day. Both of them were representative men, and types of the self-styled philosophic spirit which exhibited the bitterest hostility to the doctrines of the cross, rebelling vehemently against that union of humility and love which is the elementary conception of Christian morals.

At Philippi the speculations of the two men led them to the same characteristic end. Black despair, a passion abhorrent to the Christian heart, seized alike upon the self-mortifying Stoic and the self-indulgent Epicurean. At the first reverse of the Republican army Cassius killed himself, and was extolled by his friend as the last of the Romans. Brutus attempted another struggle with the conquerors; but when defeat seemed inevitable, he bade a companion take his sword and hold it firmly by the hilt, that he might throw himself upon the blade and die. Thus perished Brutus, the most formidable of the enemies of the Cæsars and their despotism.

II. A few years later a Divine Infant was born in a stable at Bethlehem; and within a century the foundation of a Christian Church was laid at Philippi, to which the apostle of the Gentiles, then a prisoner in Imperial Rome, despatched his affectionate letter to console the believers in the afflictions which they endured for the sake of Christ.

III. It is difficult to imagine any contrast between two different aspects of human life more complete than that which is presented by the scenes enacted at Philippi, when the old Gentile paganism was doing its best and its worst for man's social condition, and that of the quiet Christian community to whom St. Paul wrote this most interesting and touching Epistle.

None of his letters contain more ample testimonies to those elements in St. Paul's character which fitted him for the work to which the Divine will called him. Nowhere do we feel more distinctly that we are reading the words of a man to whom self-consciousness was an infirmity absolutely unknown. This infirmity is, indeed, an especial characteristic of our modern days. The deliberate self-inspection which is cultivated even by good Christians, with a view to describing their inner life in verse or prose, to be published for the benefit of others, was a practice unheard of when the world was still young or middle-aged. And with all St. Paul's knowledge of the singularities and eccentricities of human nature, it may be questioned whether he ever formed a conception of this remarkable growth of modern civilization. And if it were possible for the Philippian Christians to have been transported into a state of society such as that which now exists in England, France, and Italy, and, above all, in Germany, their surprise at the prevalence of this spirit of self-consciousness would amount to something like bewilderment. Can it be possible, they would ask, that the authors of these introspective poems, autobiographies, and works of fiction can be men and women who understand the

Christian graces of simplicity and meekness? These old-world people could understand such vehement outpourings of passion as the poetry of Sappho, or the more refined emotionalism of Anacreon. The thirteenth century, too, would offer no incomprehensible phenomena for their study; and even our own Elizabethan writers and the men of the Italian Renaissance would not seem to the apostolic Christians to have intellects and feelings very different from their own. But as for this nineteenth century, they would confess that it was incomprehensible, and that its current phraseology represented certain ideas which to themselves were simply unknown. What do you mean, they would inquire, by a *morbid* state of feeling? And you call a certain way of looking at things *unreal*—what is that?

IV. In truth, the change that has gradually come over the modes of thinking general in civilized society is so great, that without a sustained effort we cannot do justice to those elements in the nature of St. Paul, which show themselves in everything that he wrote, and with especial force and beauty when he was writing to his beloved Philippians.

Every sentence that he has here written about himself being thus marked with his usual absolute unaffectedness, we are carried on with ever-increasing interest, as we read his self-portraiture, admitting us, as it does, into the innermost recesses of as pure and noble a nature as was ever trained by Divine grace to live a life of self-sacrifice for others.

At this time, indeed, being now a prisoner at Rome, St. Paul was beginning to grow weary of his long and exhausting labours. He tells the Philippians that he is in a strait between two desires, drawing him in different directions. He longs for his release, that he may depart and be with Christ, which, he says, is far better. But as he thinks it will be for their good if he should live a little longer, he is ready to remain while his Master has occasion for him.

The manner, again, in which he thanks the Philippians for the contribution in money which they had sent him, exhibits just the same simple-minded cordiality, and that union of affectionateness and dignity which constituted a chief source of his wonderful influence wherever he was known. Hearing of his imprisonment at Rome, and thinking that he might want money, the Philippian Christians made a collection among themselves, and sent their contributions to him by the hands of Epaphroditus, who is mentioned by Theodoret as being the bishop of the Philippian Church. On receiving their offerings, and hearing also of their devout lives, and the courage with which they withstood persecution of every kind, he wrote to thank them for their gift, and to pour forth all his personal love for them, calling their attention at the same time to the great doctrines of the gospel, the knowledge of which was the inestimable blessing of their lives, as it was of his own.

V. The Philippian Church seems, further, to have been one of those communities which were but slightly troubled by the pretensions of the Judaizing converts. These latter appear to have been less numerous than the believers of Gentile origin. But, however this may be, there is but one sentence in this Epistle in which St. Paul warns the Philippians against the plausible theory which in some Churches proved so formidable an obstacle to the cultivation of the spiritual life, and of peace and harmony among the believers.

VI. Judging from the Epistle as a whole, we cannot help concluding that the Philippian Church was one of the happiest and most cultivated of the Christian communities of the apostolic period. And it is easy to picture to ourselves the delight with which this letter was received, and read and pondered over from week to week in the quiet gatherings of the believers. We, indeed, familiar as we are with the whole treasure of the great apostle's writings, can scarcely understand what it was to these devout and often persecuted men and women to receive one of these letters.

Yet it is worth while to make the effort, and try to understand the condition of persons whose early associations and whose circumstances were so unlike our own; when there were no dogmatic creeds in existence, and everything that was known of Jesus

Christ was from unwritten tradition only, and believers like those in Philippi lived upon their recollections of what St. Paul had personally taught them a few years before.

When we have done this, we shall be able to understand the emotion that moved the faithful Church when it was known that a messenger had come from Rome with a letter from their much-loved teacher in his prison. We can imagine the eager questions which one put to another concerning the contents of the letter, until it was read aloud in their assembly; how they pressed the messenger himself for news of their friend, about his health, his needs, the severity of his imprisonment, and the progress of the appeal to the imperial tribunal which had taken him to Rome.

Then, when they had heard the letter, and well weighed every part of it, and not the least anxiously his acknowledgment of the gift they had sent him, their thoughts would be fixed upon the words in which he gave utterance to his wish for death. How natural it was, they would feel, that this should be his desire; and how natural, too, that he should take them into his confidence without scruple, and with all his usual straightforwardness and directness! How could he help wishing for his Master's summons? It was impossible that it should be otherwise.

To us, in our modern days, it is not so easy to enter into the apostle's real desire for death as it was to the believers who would suffer so much by what would be his gain. To us, indeed, a desire for death is not an unknown thing, even when accompanied with an unhesitating submission to the Divine will. But, then, when good Christians desire death, it is because of their weariness under the sorrows that afflict them, and which have made all enjoyment of life impossible.

Not so with St. Paul. For very many years— ever since his conversion, in fact—he had renounced all thought of life as a period of possible enjoyment. He had been living for the sake of others, and for their sake only. With us, on the contrary, if it rested with ourselves to alter our circumstances, life would not be, what it often is, a wearisome burden or a miserable failure.

The Philippians, however, knew what St. Paul's life was, which they could partly understand from their experience of what it was to be a Christian in the midst of a cruel and contemptuous heathen society. To them it was not a matter for surprise that their much-loved friend should at last be worn out. Even the most heroic natures are at length exhausted, and it was not for them to complain when their spiritual guide frankly confessed that he should be glad if it were the will of God that his labours should be ended.

How genuine was the resignation to the Divine will which the Philippians shared with their teacher cannot easily be understood by ourselves. We should, however, frame a very imperfect conception of the actual state of things in the apostolic Churches like that of Philippi if we measured their ideal of a Christian life by our own. With us it is usually our aim to extract as much enjoyment from life as we can without falling into sin. But the Philippians passed their days and nights in a perpetual conflict, not knowing what was next to befall them, and in their degree sharing the apostle's own feelings when he said, "To me to live is Christ." The one great comfort of their lives, and the source of their joy and peace, was their faith in Christ and their love of Christ in the midst of a persecuting world.

Hence there grew up among them a certain healthy, manly, cheerful tone of mind, not common in our easy-going civilisation, which kept them ready for every emergency. It was this vigorous serenity which supported the believers in Rome when the horrible cry, "Christianos ad leones!" struck upon their ears, yelled forth from the savage multitudes assembled in the Coliseum, to whom no sight was so sweet as that of the mangled limbs of a dying Christian, torn by the savage lions from the sands of Africa. And these memories it is that rise in our thoughts when we stray amidst the now silent amphitheatres of Verona and Rome. Still the echoes of the old cry, "Christianos ad leones!" seem to linger among the crumbling walls and arches, and to tell us what it was to be a faithful Christian eighteen hundred years ago.

Yes; those days are past. The world is eighteen centuries older. Is it eighteen centuries wiser or better? Who among us would exchange his own age, which has made him what he is, for any other epoch in the years gone by? Nevertheless, if only for the purposes of study, it is well to make these letters of the great apostle our daily companions, and to attempt by their help to realize the conditions of a past civilization, and the hopes and joys of a generation so little akin to our own. Then, when we have really recalled those scenes of blood and passion, at once so horrible and so glorious, we shall know indeed what it was to live at Philippi in the old days.

CHAPTER X.

THE EPISTLE TO PHILEMON.

1. THE Epistle to Philemon was written about the same time as the Epistle to the Philippians, while St. Paul was still a prisoner at Rome. Being addressed to a single person, it is chiefly valuable as illustrating the character of St. Paul himself. Here he appears just the same man as he shows himself on every other occasion; and we hardly know which most to admire, his simple, unaffected dignity, or the loving tenderness of his heart.

Philemon was a member of the Church at Colosse, in which he held an official position. From this Epistle it appears that he had been converted to Christianity by St. Paul, who evidently held him in high esteem for his goodness, setting aside his feelings of personal regard.

Onesimus, who brought the letter from Rome, was the servant, apparently the slave, of Philemon, from whom he had run away. At Rome he made the acquaintance of St. Paul, under whose instructions Onesimus became a Christian. Probably he was already prepossessed in favour of the religion of Christ by what he had seen in the family of Philemon, and was thus induced to go to St. Paul, especially when he found so many people flocking to see the wonderful man, concerning whom rumour spread such strange reports.

II. What kind of a person was this runaway servant we do not learn from the Epistle. But it must be remembered that the relation of a slave to his master in those days implied none of that sense of degradation with which we now associate it. At any rate, Onesimus had become a good Christian, and St. Paul at once sent him back to his old master at Colosse, carrying this letter with him.

The letter is a model of skill and good taste, and, considering the difficulty of writing such a letter, must be accepted as a proof of that astonishing versatility in the great apostle, which was one of his most striking characteristics. Philemon must have been less than an ordinary man, and, still more, less than an ordinary Christian, if he was not touched by St. Paul's appeal to his consciousness that in reality he owed to him his spiritual life, and that his father in the faith might reasonably have asked him, as an obedient son, to receive back the penitent Onesimus. But instead of doing this, St. Paul puts it to him as a favour, and undertakes himself to repay to Philemon whatever losses he may have suffered through the misconduct of his servant.

III. Studied thus by itself, this short letter impresses us afresh with the amazing variety of St. Paul's writings. Now that they are collected together as an integral portion of the New Testament, we are apt to read them so much as a whole, as to overlook their strongly-marked differences. Knowing that they teach but one gospel, and are the work of one man, we compare phrase with phrase and context with context, and arrange the result into a compendium of theology. And all this is well, provided that we do not overlook their biographical aspect.

The value of the Epistle to Philemon is therefore considerable, as a contribution to our knowledge of St. Paul's personality—a subject, it need hardly be said, of the first importance in any attempt to reproduce the actual life of the Christian Churches of the apostolic period. And, in truth, the more closely we study St. Paul's Epistles with the view of understanding the life of the time, the more vivid is the impression we receive of the personal qualities of the writer. I do not think that I exaggerate when I say that St. Paul stands almost alone, in the records of the Christian Church, as at once the most highly-gifted and the most lovable of men, as he certainly held a position unlike that of any other among the first preachers of the gospel. As an example of careful skill in writing to a friend on a delicate subject, this Epistle to Philemon has always been held to be unsurpassed. But to estimate it correctly, it must be taken in connection with all St. Paul's other letters, and then it will be recognized as the spontaneous work of a nature, simple in all its complexity, because its animating principles were humility and love.

CHAPTER XI.

THE EPISTLE TO THE HEBREWS.

I. THERE is hardly any difficulty in determining the date when this Epistle was written, which may be assumed to be a little after the year in which St. Paul wrote to Philemon. But there is some difficulty in determining its authorship, of which nothing is said in the Epistle itself. The references to it in the writings of the Fathers leave its actual authorship open to doubt. It has been attributed to Barnabas, to Timothy, and to Apollos. Modern scholarship inclines to attribute it to Apollos.

For our present purpose the question is not very important. It is undeniable that, if not actually the composition of St. Paul, the Epistle came from one of his intimate associates, and that it embodies the substance of the doctrinal teaching which he wished to enforce upon the Christian believers of Hebrew origin.

Whether the Christians thus addressed are to be regarded as the Hebrew believers generally, or as those of some one country in particular, is a further question. From the contents of the Epistle, I am myself disposed to concur in the opinion that it was the Jewish believers settled in Palestine whom the writer had mainly in view. Knowing as we do, from St. Paul's letters to local Churches, what was the kind of influence that the Jewish converts generally attempted to exercise over their brethren of Gentile origin, it would be strange indeed to find no reference to such influence in this Epistle, if it was addressed to the Hebrew believers settled in Asia Minor, Italy, or Greece. It is clear, I think, that the writer had in his mind the Jewish Christians of some district where they were numerically almost the only persons who had received the gospel. Such a district was Palestine, a province of the Roman empire, but practically inhabited only by the descendants of Judah and Benjamin.

Further, although the doctrines enforced in this Epistle are identical with those taught by St. Paul in his undoubted writings, the method by which they are here expounded would have been uninteresting, if not unintelligible, to any but thoroughly Jewish minds, more habitually accustomed to the elaborate ritual of the temple-worship at Jerusalem than would have been the case with the Jews scattered about in the countries beyond the limits of Palestine.

II. But whether or not the Epistle was especially addressed to the converted Jews in Palestine, it is certain that the highly figurative illustrations by which the mediatorial office of Christ is explained presuppose a familiarity with all the details of the Mosaic ritual which would be found in Jews alone. If we put ourselves in the place of the early believers who were educated as Gentiles, we shall see at once that they would scarcely have understood the subtle reasonings by which the writer of this Epistle shows the typical nature of the old Mosaic priesthood, and its bearing upon the sacerdotal functions of the Eternal Son, incarnate for the sins of the whole world.

III. The Epistle, then, must be studied as addressed to the Hebrew Christians of the Apostolic period, regarded simply as they were in themselves, and without reference to that narrow-minded arrogance which they often displayed towards the Gentile Christians. At the same time, that peculiar temper which the writer of this Epistle evidently regards as characteristic of the Hebrews, as such, is closely akin to that special mental fault which led them to invent the theory concerning the perpetual obligation of the law of Moses with which they harassed the Gentile believers in so many places. This temper may be briefly described as a haughty worldliness.

As a corrective of this temper, throughout this Epistle, the aim of the writer is to point out the office and power of faith, as being that attitude of the mind which alone befits men in their intercourse with God, and in their interpretation of the facts of human life. Faith is here defined as the substance of things hoped for, the evidence of things not seen. It is in this sense that the word is used by our Lord, when He says to the disciples, " If ye have faith as a grain of mustard seed, ye shall say to this mountain, Remove hence to yonder place, and it shall remove, and nothing shall be impossible to you."

By faith, then, as the term is employed in this Epistle, the Christian, under the gospel dispensation, like every good man in times past, views all things as they are in reality, not mistaking the shadow for the substance, nor the type for the thing typified, nor the temporal for the eternal, nor the physical laws of the universe for a power greater than God who creates those laws. He lives in the midst of a visible world, never forgetting that what he sees and hears is a species of veil, behind which are all the realities of the spiritual world, with God who is the Creator and Lord of all. In this God he trusts with undoubting faith, distrusting himself and repudiating himself, but confidently relying, with perfect humility, upon the power, the promises, and the goodness of Him who is unseen.

IV. Thus it was that the saints of old, many of whom are specified by name in this Epistle, triumphed over the difficulties which beset them. And thus it is that the Christian realizes all that is involved in his relation to the risen and glorified Jesus, and to the saints who have already entered into their rest, the inhabitants of the heavenly Jerusalem. This relationship, being not an empty metaphor, but a practical reality, is briefly described towards the end of the Epistle in the words, "Ye are come to Mount Sion, and to the city of the living God, the heavenly Jerusalem, and to an innumerable company of angels, to the general assemblage and Church of the firstborn, who are written in heaven, and to God the Judge of all, and to the spirits of just men made perfect, and to Jesus the Mediator of the New Covenant, and to the blood of sprinkling, which speaketh better things than that of Abel" (chap. xii. 22–24).

V. Faith being thus the necessary action of the mind when it contemplates its own relation towards its Creator, its function is pointed out with especial emphasis by St. Paul in the Epistle to the Romans, where he explains that man is justified by faith, and not by the works of the law, as was imagined by the corrupt Judaism of the time.

VI. The impression which the Epistle to the Hebrews thus leaves upon us is much the same as that produced by the letters in which St. Paul places before us the characteristic temper, or $\mathring{\eta}\theta$os, of the Hebrew race in general. They were a proud, unspiritual, worldly minded people, who would have made a bargain with God Himself, and claimed as a right what could only have been granted them as a free gift. Even when their conversion to the faith of Christ had brought them under the power of its morality, and taught them humility and love, the stubbornness, hardness, and pride which were inherent in the children of Abraham made it necessary for their spiritual guides to insist again and again upon the cultivation of those Christian graces which were most alien to their national tendencies.

VII. The perpetuity of character in the Hebrew race is, indeed, one of those psychological and physiological phenomena which seem irreconcilable with our accepted theories on the laws of healthy vitality. To this very day the Jew remains very much what he was in the days of the Pharaohs. From the time when the descendants of Abraham were organized into twelve separate tribes by the authority of Moses after their escape from bondage in Egypt, they have exhibited a tenacity of existence and character under circumstances which would have proved fatal to any other variety of mankind. Even during their bondage in Egypt they seem to have given proofs of an unparalleled tenacity and unity of disposition which made them formidable to their masters. Who but Moses, himself a pure Hebrew, could have controlled such a people as he had to deal with during their long wanderings in the desert before the land of Canaan was finally reached and conquered?

Then followed the many centuries of national life, under an elaborate system of rigid tribal division, and of marriage regulations involving the intermarriage of blood-relations, which would have reduced to an effete feebleness any people of the prolific Aryan stock. Few, comparatively, as were these men and women of Semitic origin, and practising, moreover, polygamy and family concubinage—customs the reverse of invigorating to any people which adopts them—still the children of Israel have gone on from century to century, fighting their enemies, surviving a second captivity, preserving their old law, giving birth to all the prophetic, poetic, and devotional literature enshrined in the Old Testament, and, since the triumph of Christianity, resisting successfully every attempt to convert them by persecution, or to crush out their unconquered vitality.

VIII. In all this wonderful history one fact stands out with startling prominence. St. Paul refers to this fact in his second letter to the Corinthians. "Even unto this day," he says, "when Moses is read, the veil is upon their heart. Nevertheless, when it shall turn to the Lord, the veil shall be taken away" (2 Cor. iii. 15, 16).

And the more we reflect upon the contents of this Epistle to the Hebrews, the more impossible we find it to forget the fact, that from the times of the apostles to our own the Jewish mind has remained impervious to the Christian interpretation of the law of Moses and of the Psalms and prophecies of the Old Testament. During the apostolic period, with all the bitterness which the Hebrew race displayed towards the preachers of the gospel, it yielded many converts to their arguments, though apparently not nearly so many as those who were converted from heathenism.

But since those early times, with few exceptions, the Jewish race has been as little moved by argument as by persecution. It is true that here and there a sincere conversion has occurred, and does now occur; but these are so few that they serve only to draw attention to the general fact described by St. Paul in the words, "When Moses is read, the veil is upon their heart."

IX. To every thoughtful mind the phenomenon is unquestionably one of the most inexplicable in ecclesiastical history, though it can partly be explained by those peculiarities of hereditary temperament to which I have been calling attention. The psychological unity of the race of Israel, from the time of Abraham downwards, unparalleled in the records of any Indo-Germanic nation, goes some way to account for its attitude towards Christianity since the period when it gave thousands of believers and many martyrs to the faith of Christ crucified.

X. But why is it so no longer? Why are sincere conversions from Judaism so rare, that argumentatively they may be set down as practically non-existent? The question cannot be answered by any of the ordinary theories which are brought forward to account for men's actions. The Jews are a phenomenon in modern society of the strangest kind. Why are they what they are? And why do they everywhere awaken in tolerant and enlightened minds such a mixture of respect, admiration, and aversion? They are among the chief financiers of the world; they are everywhere loyal citizens; their intellectual capacities are great and varied.

But see how strange is the position which they hold in European life. I will not insist on their legal status in a country like Roumania, where the people are uncouth and only partially civilized, and the aristocracy one of the most dissolute of oligarchies. Nor must too much stress be laid upon the anti-Jewish ferocities of Muscovite towns and villages. What seems inexplicable is the bitterness with which the Hebrew race is regarded by many of the best-educated and tolerant people in Germany, the very land of free thought—a feeling which bears no likeness to anything in this country, though it is not to be denied that even here the feelings of the most liberal-minded people are not very friendly where Jews are concerned.

Is it not the case, then, that everywhere there lurks in most people's minds an uncomfortable suspicion that there is something radically dangerous in the hereditary Jewish nature? Is there, or is there not, a supernatural aspect to this singular feeling towards a race who seem so little to deserve this almost universal dislike? I do not pretend to answer the question with any dogmatic positiveness. But I see no way of reconciling the fact with the ordinary facts of human life, except by supposing that there does exist some hidden reason for this continued alienation, only to be understood by its connection with what St. Paul said when he wrote to the Corinthians, that "when Moses is read, the veil is upon their heart."

If this is so, then we are further justified in looking forward to the fulfilment, sooner or later, of St. Paul's anticipation that the Jewish heart will "turn to the Lord;" and then the veil will be removed from the eyes so long unable to recognize the Messiah in the Son of Mary. Then, too, will the whole hereditary force of their race be devoted to the propagation of that gospel to whose claims they are still blind. Let us hope that this change in the Jewish hearts is not far distant. Whether, however, it is still far off, or whether it is near, its time of coming is one of those secrets which are known only to God Himself.

CHAPTER XII.

THE EPISTLES TO TIMOTHY.

I. THE Epistles to Timothy have a twofold interest. They are valuable as exhibiting the feelings entertained by St. Paul towards one whom he loved with the affectionateness of a father, and as illustrating the condition of the Ephesian Church, of which Timothy was the bishop. They are thus supplementary to the Epistle to the Ephesians, which was written only a few years before the First Epistle to Timothy. When St. Paul first wrote to Timothy, he was a prisoner for the first time at Rome. When he again wrote, he was once more a prisoner, and he urges Timothy to come to see him and comfort him with his presence. He foresaw his approaching martyrdom, to which he looked forward with the joy of a faithful servant about to receive his reward. The affectionateness of St. Paul's nature is strikingly brought out in his desire to see his much-loved son in the faith once more before he died.

It is not known whether Timothy was able to reach Rome before St. Paul's death. Nor is anything known with certainty concerning Timothy's own personal history during the latter part of his life, but tradition says that he too received the crown of martyrdom.

II. Of his life and difficulties at the time when St. Paul wrote to him, these two Epistles give a tolerably distinct picture. He was still a young man—very young for the difficult post to which St. Paul had appointed him. His health was not good, and he suffered from maladies for which St. Paul advised him to drink a little wine, instead of confining himself to water alone.

His task, as head of the Ephesian Church, was by no means an easy one, and he had need of all the strength and enlightenment which he had received from his careful Christian education, under his grandmother Lois and his mother Eunice. His early knowledge of the Old Testament Scriptures stood him in good stead in dealing with the peculiar questions which disturbed the peace of the Ephesian Christians, and which it is evident had no small attraction for their somewhat unstable, though devout, natures. Timothy's youth also added to his other difficulties, for no men liked to yield to the authority of a person much younger than themselves, and no little tact was required both in the treatment of those who caused scandal by open misconduct, and in the delicate handling of the susceptibilities of widows, in such matters as second marriages, and their enrolment in the number of those who were to be reckoned as widows indeed, and to be employed in some sort of supervision of the younger women, setting them a good example by cultivating sobriety in dress. Those who were recognized as real widows were, by St. Paul's directions, to be not less than sixty years of age.

III. The general fault of the Ephesian Church, when St. Paul wrote these letters, seems to have been what may be described as free living or self-indulgence. It is surprising, indeed, to learn, from the instructions given to Timothy for the appointment of bishops and deacons, that men of anything but irreproachable character might be expected sometimes to aspire to sacred offices. The virtues which St. Paul specifies as necessary qualifications for the offices of bishop and deacon are, in truth, by no means extravagantly severe. What is noticeable is the fact that he should have thought it necessary to give these detailed directions to a person like Timothy, who, though young, was eminent both for his piety and his wisdom. And the fact compels us to form a somewhat low estimate of the religious condition of the Ephesian Christians, and to contrast it with the very high estimate which St. Paul had formed of their spiritual state when he wrote his Epistle to them. The meaning of one of the directions here given to Timothy is at first sight not very obvious. St. Paul says that a bishop, and also a deacon, is to be the husband of one wife. This, of course, does not mean that to other persons polygamy was allowable, but simply that the bishops and deacons were to be men who had not been twice married. St. Paul also urges the importance of the effect of a well-governed family in a bishop's house upon the good conduct of the Church in general. A man who could not rule his own household well is declared to be unfit to govern the Church of God.

Taken in connection with the rules given on the recognition of widows who wished to be regarded as widows indeed, these directions illustrate St. Paul's views on the subject of second marriages in general, which he regards as inconsistent with devotion to any sort of spiritual office. The cares of married life, in his judgment, distract the attention of men and women alike; and he thinks that a woman who marries a second time would be happier if she remained all her life a widow.

IV. Examining these two epistles further in detail, it appears that there had grown up among the Ephesian believers one peculiar tendency for which we were little prepared, either by the narrative of St. Paul's preaching at Ephesus, as given in the Acts of the Apostles, or by the letter which he wrote to the Ephesians themselves. Many of them, it seems, now betrayed a fondness for all kinds of quibblings and straw-splittings, and for what St. Paul calls endless genealogies. Whether we are to understand by this phrase some interminable disputes as to a man's Jewish or Gentile origin, or whether it refers to some sort of family pretensions and disagreements, it is evident that the spirit which magnifies trifles and substitutes words for realities was rife in a community in which the power of the one true God had been not long before displayed in miraculous events, such as were vouchsafed to few of the infant Churches of Asia. Until we recollect what human nature is, in all ages and countries, it is almost startling to learn that these follies were common in the very city where the Christians had thrown off the worship of Diana, and God had wrought so many wonders by the hands of his apostle. Yet in this very city the minds of the believers were in so unsettled a condition that St. Paul found it necessary to remind their bishop to discourage the spread of triflings so foolish that he contemptuously described them as old wives' fables.

One special class of pretenders to eminent sanctity are described in terms which have led to the conclusion that they belonged to the Jewish sect of the Essenes, whose rigorism had an attraction for those persons who were dissatisfied alike with the worldliness and pretensions of the Pharisees and the cold-hearted scepticism of the Sadducees. It is not easy to ascertain from Josephus and other contemporary writers what were the exact opinions of the Essenes, or how far their conventual system rested upon such absurd notions as to eating and drinking as those referred to by St. Paul in writing to Timothy. At any rate, there was a marked similarity between the practice of the Essenes and the teaching of the Ephesian sectaries, who forbade marriage and denounced the use of certain kinds of food.

At the same time, it seems clear that the fundamental theories of the Manichean system had gained a footing in the Ephesian Church. According to this ingenious Oriental speculation, the awful mystery of human life, with its sufferings and moral evils, can only be explained by the hypothesis that two mighty invisible powers are always contending for the dominion of humanity, and that corporeal activity and enjoyment are the special instruments by means of which the evil power thwarts the efforts of the beneficent Power for the good of mankind. What St. Paul says of the mischievous assertions of the Ephesian sectaries undoubtedly corresponds with the speculations of Manicheism, more closely than any errors which were rife among the Jews, as far as they can be ascertained from the Gospels and the Acts of the Apostles.

V. As to St. Paul's own teaching, the Epistles to Timothy are clear and precise. With all his unconcealed views as to the greater happiness of the unmarried, when compared with the married state, he denounces absolutely all prohibitions of marriage, as such, and all abstaining from certain kinds of food, on the ground that they are unclean.

VI. On the whole, the impression left by these two Epistles as to the condition of the Ephesian

Church is not altogether very favourable. At the same time, it is to be borne in mind that, in writing to the bishop of the Church, St. Paul would naturally dwell more upon the faults to be corrected than upon the virtues to be commended. It is to be noted, too, in the directions which he gives as to the public worship of the believers, he makes no mention of any such abuses as those which he had condemned in the Corinthian Church when the Lord's Supper was celebrated, or such as are denounced in the Epistle of St. James. Whatever were the faults of the Ephesian Christians, they seem to have been tolerably free from the abominable sin of despising the poor, which was common among the Corinthians and the Jewish converts to whom St. James wrote.

VII. The Ephesian Church, again, included persons of all classes, both rich and poor, and many of the women were inordinately fond of dress and personal adornment. This fondness for dress was, however, an infirmity by no means confined to the Ephesian women. It is condemned by St. Peter in his First Epistle in terms which show that it was common enough among the Asiatic Christians in general. In both cases, the rebukes of the apostles are especially directed to the women's fondness for jewellery and for elaborate fashions in dressing their hair, reminding us of the figures of the Roman empresses in the British Museum, which exhibit a steady increase in the extravagant styles of arranging the hair, as the dynasty of the Cæsars drew nearer and nearer towards its close.

VIII. Of Timothy himself, as he prosecuted his difficult task, the two Epistles suggest a delightful picture. Still so young in years, yet so mature in goodness and wisdom, he seems to be an example for all ages of the lifelong effects of a Christian education, such as a Christian education always ought to be, and such as it might be, were all mothers and grandmothers like the wise and holy Eunice and Lois.

CHAPTER XIII.

THE EPISTLE TO TITUS.

I. THE Epistle to Titus is one of the most suggestive of St. Paul's letters. It is short, and much of it is occupied with the purely doctrinal and personal subjects which were never absent from St. Paul's thoughts. He touches, in passing, on the great truth that it was by the free and undeserved election of God that he was made a Christian and an apostle; and he points to the reappearance of Christ upon earth as an event to be practically looked for and longed for.

But, besides all this, the Epistle clearly shows what St. Paul thought of the Cretan believers, Gentiles as well as Jews. It was written to Titus, as the head of the Church in Crete, shortly after the First Epistle to Timothy. And if it is clear from this last that the young Timothy had a hard task in ruling the Ephesian Christians, it is equally clear that the position of Titus in Crete required not a little tact, wisdom, and firmness in administering the affairs of the Cretan believers.

II. St. Paul strikes the key-note to the general condition of the Cretan Church, when he quotes a well-known saying of a Greek poet, who said that the Cretans were always liars, ill-conditioned animals, and lazy gluttons. The charge must, of course, be accepted with reservation, as the exaggeration of a satirist; but that it condensed into one line the typical vices of the inhabitants of the island can hardly be doubted. They were a lively, quick, self-indulgent race, fond of wine, not caring for strict truth in their conversation, with a taste for ill-natured gossip, and liable to be taken in by pretenders and charlatans of all sorts. We gather, also, from the instructions given to Titus, that they were disposed to dispute the legal rights of the authorities in the island, apparently on the ground that they were aliens in race from themselves. The Judaizing party among the Christians seems to have been numerous and powerful, with the same result as at Ephesus, creating a fondness for verbal quibblings and genealogical disputes, to the injury of the simplicity and humble faith of the uncorrupted gospel.

III. It is to be remarked, further, from the qualifications which St. Paul desired Titus to require from the men whom he was to appoint as deacons in different cities, that, as in Ephesus, persons sometimes sought sacred offices who were given to drinking and devoted to money getting. Money getting generally seems to have been a passion with these islanders, who came of a Greek stock, not of the most distinguished or purest type.

As a whole, we cannot help concluding that the Cretan Church was materially affected by those influences of race which are to be traced so distinctly in many of the apostolic Churches. This modifying influence of hereditary personal qualities, upon belief as well as conduct, is one of the most curious psychological phenomena in the history of humanity, and nowhere is its reality more strikingly illustrated than in these numerous letters of St. Paul. And the value of the contribution thus yielded towards our knowledge of the religious life of the day is increased by the circumstance that St. Paul himself had no theories on the matter. Our modern theories on the subject of race and the hereditary transmission of different mental capacities had not in his day been invented. Nobody knew to what an extent thought and feeling are connected with the molecular activity of the brain, and still less had any theories been devised to account for the origin of species and the similarity of the brains of man and those of sundry brutes. St. Paul simply noticed the facts as he found them, and the remarkable varieties in his method of dealing with the spiritual condition of the different Churches to which he wrote are due to his freedom from any preconceived psychological system.

IV. One very important conclusion which is to be drawn from this Epistle to Titus is the support which it gives to the fundamental principle of all real Christian civilization—the principle, that is, that the family is the unit of the entire social state. Not merely in his instructions as to the ordination of deacons, but incidentally in other passages in this Epistle, we see that the idea of a well-ordered Christian household was constantly before St. Paul's mind. And this is the more remarkable, because no man ever had a clearer perception of the cares and anxieties of a married life. Only, as marriage is a divine institution and must always exist, St. Paul habitually recognizes the household as the basis of society, and he expects Christian perfection to be attained in the performance of the relative duties of husbands and wives, and of parents and their children.

And it is the more important to bear in mind this element in St. Paul's teaching, when we wish to realize the Christian life of the past, because undoubtedly the conversions both of Jews and Gentiles were sometimes confined to one or two members of a family. How far, indeed, this was the case it is not easy to ascertain; though, from the absence of any general instructions to individual believers who suffered from family persecution, it would seem that, as a rule, the conversion of one member of a family led to the conversion of the rest.

As to the general tone of the family life of the first Christians there can be no dispute—at least, if it was modelled on the teaching of St. Paul. That teaching is, indeed, somewhat distasteful both to the men and the women who may be taken as the typical creation of the last half of the nineteenth century. St. Paul's one conception of a Christian family was that of a household in which obedience was the ruling principle, both of the wife towards her husband and of children towards their parents. It was an affectionate obedience, and the authority was exercised with considerateness; but still, it was essentially obedience, and not a mock obedience disguising a real equality.

As to the typical nineteenth-century woman, who claims an equality with man, both in character and in rights, such a being never crossed the great apostle's imagination. His ideal of a Christian woman is that of a creature essentially feminine, whether as friend, wife, sister, mother, or daughter. He understood what we call female vanities well enough, and his censures of extravagance in the plaiting of hair and the wearing of jewellery show that he had a keen eye for female foibles. But of that theory which claims for women an actual equality with men, he had not the faintest conception. And when we read the names of the many women to whom he sends greetings in his different letters, we may rest assured that, whatever were their varieties of character, and whatever their gifts and their intellect, there was not one of them who bore the slightest resemblance to that eccentric product of modern civilization which we call a strong-minded woman.

V. At the same time, in forming our estimate of the general character and habits of the women of the apostolic period, allowance must be made for those peculiarities of race which prompted the special instructions which St. Paul gave to Timothy and Titus. There is no reason for assuming that the women of Ephesus and of Crete were fair representatives of the Christian women in all parts of the Roman empire. The people who were governed by Timothy and by Titus were a warm-blooded race, and their faults as well as their virtues were to some extent the result of hereditary temperament, modified by the circumstances in which they lived. So it is with ourselves to-day. All the women of the civilized world are not like English women, whether in their defects or their good qualities. The English woman, as such, is made what she is by her Anglo-Norman blood, and by the free political institutions amidst which she is nurtured. The result has been the gradual formation of a character which is often admirable and sometimes absurd, and as often excites the envy as the ridicule of the people of other countries. This character is also so deeply seated as to withstand the effects of transplantation to all parts of the world, while its peculiarities are intensified when they take root in places where the peculiar merits and demerits of our English life within its sea-girt shores are themselves intensified.

To answer, then, the important question, What

were the women like in the apostolic Churches ? we must include a wider range of life than is afforded by Ephesus and Crete, and by the converted Jewish inhabitants of Asia Minor to whom St. Peter addressed his two Epistles. Thus judged, there is every reason to conclude that the Christian women of the apostolic times were, as a rule, modest and simple in their ways, avoiding luxury and extravagance in their dress and in the management of their households, and looking for the re-appearance of Christ in this world. If they had been, in any sense, given to worldliness, they would not have been the mothers, wives, or sisters of martyrs; or themselves, as they sometimes were, martyrs also. This test of martyrdom is, indeed, conclusive as to the daily life of the women in the days of persecution. Martyrs do not come from the households where foolish and frivolous women give the tone to the whole family. And one almost shudders to think of the probable effects of a real persecution upon the members of our modern households, influenced by the daily and hourly guidance of the multitude of mothers and sisters who represent the self-glorifying religious world of to-day.

VI. One other question occurs to the mind, as we close our examination of the Epistles of St. Paul. What would be his view of the Christian civilization of this country at the present time ? I have failed in my attempt to represent the great apostle as a living personality to my readers, if I have left them under an impression that he was a man who would judge the Christians of the first century by one test, and those of the nineteenth by another.

Most undoubtedly he would apply his old twofold test to the England of to-day. He would inquire how far our legislation and our public and private social institutions tended to promote the knowledge of Christ crucified, and whether the men and women who profess themselves Christians habitually live like persons who are convinced that they are called to be holy, being chosen to that end by the eternal foreknowledge and predestination of God, under which same conviction they constantly look for the return of their Divine Master to this visible world. To St. Paul's mind, all other considerations would be trifles and comparatively uninteresting. He would walk about London as he walked about Athens, perhaps with the same sympathy which he there felt for those who worshipped the goddess of wisdom and the unknown God; but possibly with the same feelings which were kindled in him at Ephesus, where they worshipped Diana, or at Corinth, where they worshipped Venus, the goddess of unholy love.

Still more keen and searching would be his inquiries into the reality of our religious life, when he found Bibles in every decent house, and his own letters in Greek in the hands of almost all educated men, while he saw that the poor were crowded into dens of misery unknown to the ancient world, and the streets recalled the pleasure haunts of Corinth and the secret infamies of Tiberius Cæsar. Can we doubt what would be the conclusions that he would draw from what he saw and heard? And can we help wondering whether, in the good Providence of God, another St. Paul will ever be given to the world?

CHAPTER XIV.

THE EPISTLE OF ST. JAMES.

I. THE writer of this Epistle was James, the son of Alphæus, sometimes called James the Less, to distinguish him from the other apostle of the same name, who was the son of Zebedee. He was a kinsman of our Lord, probably a cousin, the Greek word used by St. Paul implying some sort of actual consanguinity. As far as any indications of his character can be gathered from this Epistle, we can clearly trace the peculiar personal influence which an early intimacy with the Divine Son of the ever-virgin mother would exercise upon a mind naturally sweet and humble, such as we conceive to have been that of the devout Simeon, who uttered his *Nunc Dimittis* when he received the Holy Infant in his arms in the Temple.

The Epistle is addressed to the Jewish converts generally. And it is to be noticed that they are addressed as the *twelve* tribes, either because some few descendants of the lost ten tribes were still to be found among the descendants of Judah and

Benjamin, or because the old conception of the Israelites as consisting of twelve tribes was most familiar to the Jewish households of the day.

The contents of the Epistle suggest the recollection that the writer was a poor man, very devout and humble, but without the ardent enthusiasm of St. Paul, as he was without his keen and cultivated intellect. He had a fondness for finding comparisons in inanimate objects to illustrate spiritual truths, twice drawing his illustrations from seafaring matters, as when he compares the action of the tongue upon a man's whole life to that of the rudder in shaping the course of a vessel at sea.

II. What his fellow-countrymen, the Jews, were really like he knew very well, and his censures upon their love of riches enable us to complete the picture drawn by St. Paul of the characteristics of that wonderful people, even when converted to the faith of Christ. He does not analyze the pretensions of the Judaizing theorists with St. Paul's acute logic. He is a simple man, and he merely looks at facts as they presented themselves, and he tests them by the lessons he had learnt from his Divine Master. He sees that the Jewish Christians are given to glorying in what they called their faith, but to his eyes they seem to care more for money than for anything else. He goes into their assemblies for the worship of God, and there he sees all the best places reserved for the rich and well-dressed, and the poor and ill-clad thrust into the worst seats.

Against this scandalous abuse he remonstrates, not vehemently, for he is never vehement, but with that gentle seriousness which has more force than any strength of words.

III. So, too, when he has to notice other faults, resulting from the intense pride and worldliness of the Hebrew race, he does not argue, but simply points out what are the duties of a Christian in his own calm way, and with that simplicity of definition which results from the transparent simplicity of his own mind, and which gives to many passages in his Epistle a concentrated force not surpassed by anything in all the other Epistles. Even when he has to remind the self-satisfied Jews that the faith in which they trusted was not faith at all, but a mere dead intellectual formality, he still writes in the same unimpassioned, paternal tone, recalling, if it may be said with reverence, the manner in which Jesus Himself taught His disciples.

IV. Apart, however, from the circumstance that this Epistle was specially addressed to the believers of Hebrew origin, there is no reason for thinking that its warnings were not applicable, though perhaps less generally, to the Christians of Gentile birth. The infirmities which led to the corruptions here condemned are too deeply seated in human nature to make it credible that the poor Gentile Christians were not as often neglected and looked down upon by their wealthier brethren as were the Jewish believers themselves. Nothing, too, that St. James here condemns was more scandalous than the distinctions between rich and poor in the celebration of the Lord's Supper, which St. Paul denounces in the Corinthian believers, without drawing any contrast between the Jewish and the Gentile sections of the Church.

So, too, it is only because men are men that they are prone to rest satisfied with their religious creed or faith, however dead it is and unproductive of love and all good works. The Epistle of St. James is, in fact, applicable to every age and to the wealthy believers of every race. The unpleasant truths which it quietly sets forth are echoed in the secret consciences of so many persons making loud professions of religious zeal, that we can hardly be surprised when its value is depreciated by a class of critics who understand neither St. Paul nor St. James.

V. Regarded as a means for estimating the character of St. James himself, the Epistle, short as it is, furnishes a picture of a noble, saintly nature, strong in its loving faith, patient under persecution, and habitually looking for the return of the Master to this world in His glory. It is a beautiful picture; not, perhaps, kindling in us the same personal sympathy which St. Paul's letters awaken, but moving our hearts with a very real affection. It is interesting, too, to remember that St. James was the only one of the apostles, besides St. Peter, with whom St. Paul had any conversation when he went up to Jerusalem after his conversion (Galatians i. 19). And we can understand the soothing influence of his devout and simple nature upon the ardent young convert. When St. James wrote his Epistle, many years had gone by since that first meeting at Jerusalem, and St. Paul was now on the eve of martyrdom. But they had spent their lives in the service of the same Master; and now, though eighteen centuries have passed away, they still live by their writings in our grateful memories. They themselves are in their eternal homes.

CHAPTER XV.

THE EPISTLES OF ST. PETER.

I. THE Epistles of St. Peter do not supply many details of the life of the apostolic Churches, but they deepen our perception of the extent to which the individual personality of each apostle is reflected in the letters that he wrote. In this way they add distinctness to our conceptions of the actual existence of the Christians of the time, which would be very imperfect if we had nothing more than a kind of shadowy vision of the teachers who lived among them, or from time to time addressed to them those communications which have come down to ourselves.

The value of the New Testament Epistles in thus enabling us to understand the peculiar characters of their writers cannot easily be overstated. The men to whom Jesus Christ committed the work of propagating His religion were not mere unintelligent instruments, giving forth sounds like a trumpet when it is played upon. They were as unlike one another as they could well be. When, by the teaching of

Jesus and the operation of an inward spiritual power, they became new men, both in their beliefs and in the motives which swayed their conduct, their original intellectual and emotional natures remained the same as before, and they exhibited the same varieties of type, as living men, as are exhibited by devout persons to-day.

All this is so obvious, when plainly stated, that it seems unnecessary to insist upon it. But it is not so. No book has suffered more than the New Testament from being read as a collection of documents rather than as the record of the lives, the beliefs, and the sufferings of human beings in all things like ourselves. Thus, too, its extraordinary value as a practical guide has been obscured; and people go about with it in their possession, almost as unconscious of its hidden energy as a child, playing in the fields of Golconda, who picks up an unpolished diamond, and, taking it for a common stone, tosses it backwards and forwards in a game with his companions.

II. Another consequence of this general forgetfulness of the differences of character in the writers of the Epistles is, that we are thus led to overlook the conclusions to be drawn from the absolute identity of the doctrines they teach and the morality they inculcate. This unanimity becomes the more striking, the more their letters are examined in connection with the individuality of the writers themselves.

Occasionally, for want of recollection of these facts, issues have been raised, and controversies have raged, which, but for the seriousness of the questions involved, would be almost ludicrous. Such, for instance, is the contrast which has been drawn between the teaching of St. Paul and St. James on the subject of justification by faith, while in reality their teachings are identical.

III. Regarded, then, as a contribution to our knowledge of St. Peter's own character, these two Epistles seem to be precisely what we should have expected from the apostle whose virtues and whose failings appear so distinctly in the Gospel narratives. From the day when he was first called to leave his occupation as a fisherman and become a fisher of men, up to the moment when the eyes of the Master whom he had just denied were turned upon him in sad reproach, bringing him to instant and bitter repentance, the Gospels place before us a bold, vigorous, warm-hearted, impulsive nature; manly, self-reliant, and courageous, notwithstanding his one terrible experience of the truth of the teaching that pride goes before a fall.

Just such he appears in his two Epistles. As compositions, they have no pretensions to polish of style; but they are forcible and straightforward, abounding in sentences which linger in the memory and touch the feelings. Being written about A.D. 64, when the persecutions of the Christians were on the increase, St. Peter's special aim is to encourage and instruct the believers in their trials. And he does this with his characteristic fervour, and with all those unaffected expressions of love for his Master and confidence in His power and goodness which we should expect from the living Peter of the Gospels, converted from his old Jewish exclusiveness by a special vision from heaven.

He says but little of himself personally, just mentioning that he held the office of a deacon, when he is pointing out to deacons in general the duties which their office involved. The most important passage of a personal nature is that in which he refers to the letters of St. Paul, with many of which, if not with all of them, he was evidently acquainted. He calls him his beloved brother, and adds that in his letters there were some things hard to understand, which ignorant and unstable persons perverted to their own injury. Whether he meant that his brother apostle's methods of reasoning were such as he himself found it difficult to enter into, or whether he only thought them difficult to ignorant and unstable minds, we can well imagine that he did not always follow their subtle and profound lines of argument without an effort. He was born and bred a fisherman; and though both he and the accomplished scholar whom God had made the apostle of the Gentiles preached the same gospel, their methods of teaching were different.

Now and then, it is true, there is almost a verbal similarity between the expressions used by the two writers. St. Peter's reference to the foreknowledge and election of God, which had made the believers what they were, is almost in its very words identical with St. Paul's references to the same doctrine. Another agreement is to be noticed in their way of treating a subject of a very simple kind. Both of them censure the prevailing fondness of many of the women for luxury in dress, especially mentioning the elaborate dressing of the hair and the wearing of jewellery as unbecoming the modesty and simplicity of persons who were the followers of Jesus Christ.

IV. There is not much difficulty in determining the meaning of the term "strangers," to whom these two Epistles are addressed. St. Peter calls them the strangers scattered throughout Pontus, Galatia, Cappadocia, Asia, and Bithynia—meaning, no doubt, the converted Jews who had settled in Asia Minor, under the stress of persecution in their own country. Some error, however, has crept into the enumeration of the countries specified, which are all of them provinces of Asia Minor, while there is no district known as "Asia." Possibly this word was substituted for Thracia, in the course of the various copyings which the original manuscript underwent as time wore on.

However this may be, those Asiatic converted Jews seem, in St. Peter's judgment, to have felt keenly the persecutions they had to endure, besides the ordinary trials and temptations which beset those who strive to live up to a Christian standard in this weary world. Like the various Churches addressed by St. Paul, they found in the conviction that they were the elect of God, not a pretext for sin, but an incentive to a pious life.

And thus, though these two Epistles do not add materially to the details of the early Christian life, they deepen our conviction of the contrast between the realities of ancient times and those of our own. It was one thing to be a Christian in the days of St. Peter and St. Paul ; it is quite another thing to be a Christian in our own days. For myself, I suppose that I only express the feelings of most people, when I say that I think it is easier, on the whole, to be a good Christian to-day than it was in those primitive times, even though the believers had the advantage of the personal guidance of the apostles.

At the same time, we are entitled to claim kinship with those noble souls, men and women who kept the faith amidst trials from which our more timid natures shrink, even in thought. And with these feelings in our mind, we conclude our examination of St. Peter's exhortations to the faithful of his day, by once more reading what St. John says of him at the end of his Gospel. Surely, in the sacred narratives there are not many things more full of pathos than the words in which the risen Lord foretells to His devoted and penitent servant by what death he should glorify God. And as we read the narrative, in our silent hearts we repeat the adoring cry of the *Te Deum*, " Te martyrum candidatus laudat exercitus." In all that white-robed army of martyrs, what voice is now sweeter in the ears of the glorified Jesus than that of the repentant saint on whom He cast that look of sad reproach in the hour of His humiliation and death ?

CHAPTER XVI.

THE EPISTLES OF ST. JOHN.

1. As we finish the concluding sentences of the first of these Epistles, our thoughts recall the interior of a large upper chamber in Jerusalem, and all that there took place on the evening of the Passover, thirty-five years before this Epistle was written. We see a table, showing that the Passover supper is nearly ended. At the table are placed twelve men, all but one with grave and thoughtful countenances, attentive to every word that falls from their Master, as He speaks of His approaching death. One of their number, who is placed next to Him, and even leans upon His breast, watches Him with an indescribable look of loving tenderness.

Several hours have passed away, and the Master is dying in agony upon a cross on Mount Calvary. Before He dies, He utters a few occasional words, for even in His anguish His thoughts are in heaven as well as upon earth; and among these last words are those addressed to His mother Mary, who stands by His cross with breaking heart, and to the disciple who leaned on His breast at the supper, and who now stands before Him, by His mother's side. To that beloved disciple He commits the care of His mother; and, when all is over, the disciple takes her to his own home.

II. The Epistles of St. John are the natural utterances of this beloved disciple. The thirty-five years that have passed since the voice of Jesus sounded in his ears have not clouded his memory or chilled his heart. He is still the disciple whom Jesus loved, only now he is an old man, with all the fruits of a long experience of all the perversities and weaknesses of human nature in those to whom he has taught the gospel of his Master. And now, before the infirmities of age have at last enfeebled him, he writes these letters as his offering to the followers of the Master who has given him this long life to be spent in His service.

As a contribution to our knowledge of the life of the apostolic Christians, St. John's Epistles must be taken in connection with his accounts of the condition of the seven Churches in Asia Minor, which are given in the opening chapters of the Apocalypse, in which St. John records the visions which he saw in the island of Patmos. However obscure are many parts of these revelations of the future destiny of the Church and the world, there is no difficulty in understanding the warnings addressed to the seven Churches. Ephesus, Smyrna, Pergamos, Thyatira, Philadelphia, Sardis, and Laodicea stand out distinctly before us, as they appeared to St. John himself; and their characteristic virtues and faults must be regarded as proofs of the extent to which they had obeyed or neglected the teaching of St. John's Epistles.

It is evident that in most of these communities there was a tendency to fall away before the subtle insinuations of speculative reasoners who were not content simply to adore Jesus as God. In this respect the Asiatic Churches seem to have been more disposed to go astray than the generality of the communities of Christian believers. At the same time, it is to be remembered that we have no account of the condition of the Churches to whom St. Paul wrote, subsequent to his letters to Timothy and Titus, which only give us an insight into the affairs of Ephesus and Crete.

To the beloved disciple, who had leaned upon the breast of Him whom he worshipped as God manifest in the flesh, any speculations that tended to obscure a simple belief in the reality of the Incarnation must have been indescribably abhorrent, and if anything could have embittered his own loving nature it was this appearance of the delusion which made men turn against the Divine Lord whom he loved. These accounts of the seven Churches further confirm the conclusion gathered from many parts of St. Paul's Epistles as to the tendency to licentiousness, so difficult to eradicate from many of the believers, brought up in all the voluptuous self-indulgence of Asiatic heathenism. In the people of Laodicea another characteristic is severely censured. They seem to have given up all serious care for either virtue or vice, and their name has become proverbial for a lukewarmness, a temper of mind which the speaker in the Apocalyptic vision condemns with an unsparing rigour, incomprehensible to those who do not know the hopelessness of attempting to move those who are neither cold nor hot, but merely indifferent, in any cause, however good and great.

CHAPTER XVII.

THE EPISTLE OF JUDE.

THE general impression that we derive from this brief but vigorously-expressed letter, is in many respects the same as that which is produced by the Epistles of St. John and the warnings addressed to the seven Churches of Asia Minor in the Apocalypse. It was written about the same time as St. John's Epistles, and must be regarded as practically illustrating the chief faults of the time. The difference between the characters of the two writers is very evident, but in both of them we observe a keen sense of the dangers, both to faith and morals, which beset the believers to whom they wrote. The burden of the Epistle of Jude is the inevitable punishment which follows a falling-away from the gospel, as first received by those who embrace it. How far these strictures are to be taken as implying any extensive changes in the beliefs and lives of the apostolic Churches generally, it is not easy to determine. Probably the Epistle represents the zeal and the fears of the writer's heart, rather than his deliberate judgment as to actual facts. The severity of its tone certainly does not prepare us for the heroic constancy displayed by the Christians of the day, when the great persecution under Nero tried their faithfulness to the utmost. And the chief inference to be drawn from the Epistle is the profound reality of the struggle that went on in the minds of the believers, resulting in the defection of the few, and the triumphant victory of the many, over the most subtle of snares and the most terrible of deaths.

CHAPTER XVIII.

GENERAL CHARACTER OF THE APOSTOLIC CHURCH.

I. THE history of the apostolic Church, as gathered from the materials supplied by the Epistles in the New Testament, extends over a period of about sixteen years. We are thus in possession of abundant information concerning the details of the life of the various Christian Churches from A.D. 52, when the first Epistle to the Thessalonians was written, down to the beginning of the great persecution under Nero.

Practically, this Christian life was almost confined to Greece, Palestine, Asia Minor, a few islands in the Mediterranean, and, in Italy, to Rome. A glance at the map of the world, as known to the ancients, shows how small was the region, judged by mere size, to which Christianity had penetrated during the first thirty-five years after the death of its Divine Founder. But in the conquests it had thus made it had captured the very heart and head of the human race. With the exception of those districts in the farther East, where, in the cradle of the great Aryan, afterwards the Indo-Germanic race, Brahmanism and Buddhism held undisputed sway, the religion of the cross had been planted in the chief centres of civilization, and the temples of mythological deities were rocking to their foundations. Everywhere, in the midst of wondering and hostile populations, crowds of men and women were living, looking like other men and women, and following the same callings as their fellow-citizens, but asserting that the Son of a virgin mother, born in an obscure town in Judæa, and crucified at the instigation of his fellow-countrymen, was the Son of the one only true God, and would one day return to reward those who believed in Him.

To their heathen neighbours these Christians seemed all very much like one another, and possessed with one incomprehensible fanaticism; but yet in many respects their separate communities differed not a little. Still, as Christians, they were all agreed in certain characteristic beliefs, some of which would have been peculiarly odious to their heathen neighbours, even if correctly understood; and which, being only imperfectly comprehended, did make them formidable in the eyes of those who watched them with mingled jealousy and fear.

II. Of these universal Christian beliefs, none was more intolerable to the heathen world than the conviction that each local Church was an integral portion of one vast spiritual kingdom, governed by its own laws, and ruled over by the risen and glorified Jesus. Of this fundamental element in the faith of the apostolic Christians, the heathen could only master the conception that the Church was a powerful kingdom, and therefore to be dreaded. It was nothing to them that it had none of the externals of royalty, none of the pomp and magnificence and the emblems of power which they saw in the sovereignty of the Cæsars. To them the Christian was not a mere dreaming fanatic, a sort of peevish puritan, who would take no part in drunken revels or licentious pleasures of any kind. He was a revolutionist, a disturber of society; he was not only a disagreeable, he was a dangerous man.

To the unconverted Jews this belief in a universal spiritual kingdom was as odious as it was to the idolatrous Gentile. The Christian was in their eyes a marked man wherever he was found. As he went about his private affairs, he was the living embodiment of a denial of the Jewish aspirations after a temporal Messiah. Every word that he uttered concerning the glories of the heavenly Jerusalem was equivalent to an assertion that the Jewish expectations of a triumphant Jerusalem, rich, glorious, and free, were doomed to disappointment; and the Jew therefore hated the Christian with a bitterness all his own.

This universal aversion of Jews and heathens was further intensified by the expectation of the return of Jesus to this visible world which was general in the apostolic Church. That he would certainly thus return, perhaps in a few years, was undoubtedly the conviction of the Christians who were taught by St. Paul and the other writers of the Epistles. Jew and Gentile could alike understand what the Christian meant when he stated his expectation that perhaps before a year was over the Son of Mary, who had been crucified in Judæa, might appear and take possession of the world, with all His saints about Him. Here was an announcement which appealed to the senses of the non-Christian inhabitants of every town and village where Christians were to be found. It is, therefore, no matter of surprise when we find, as time wore on, that however the Christians were tolerated in the apostolic period, they were surrounded by latent feelings of hostility, which quickly broke out into a flame when excited by any fresh stimulus to popular passion.

There was no difficulty, again, in knowing who were Christians and who were not. The Church which the Christians believed in was a visible Church. The theory that has been invented in modern times, which regards the Church of Christ as made up of pious souls, bound together in an invisible union, was unknown in the apostolic Church itself. People, it was universally held, were made Christians by being baptized, when they received that special gift of the Holy Ghost which enabled them to fulfil the law of God. Every one, therefore, in Corinth, or Rome, or Ephesus, knew who were Christians as well as they knew who were Jews and who were worshippers of Venus or Diana. There might be bad Christians, as well as good Christians; and we cannot doubt that those who showed themselves false to their faith by indulging in gross sin, excited far more contempt than sympathy in their unbelieving neighbours.

One other element in the belief of the Christians of those days was of a more secret nature, but, whenever it came to the ears of their unconverted companions, aggravated not a little the dislike already entertained towards the followers of Jesus. This was their belief that it was by the election of God, and by His free grace, that they had been chosen out of a sinful and miserable world, to be His saints upon earth, and the inheritors of eternal life. Even when stated with the utmost humility and charity towards all men, this doctrine is apt to create irritation in many minds amongst ourselves. What, then, must have been its effect on the unbelieving Jews and pagans, already sufficiently disposed to denounce the arrogance of these insolent Christians? It was nothing to them that the Christians held that predestination to eternal happiness involved a predestination to a life of holiness, after the pattern set by Jesus Christ Himself, and that those who were not made holy were not of the number of the elect. It was enough to arouse the anger of Jew and Gentile, to hear these Christians professing themselves the elect of God, according to His eternal foreknowledge and omnipotent will.

The anger aroused by this doctrine of election was further intensified when it was remarked that those who held it were for the most part persons in a humble social position. Some of them were rich and well dressed, and patrician in their family connections. Not so the greater number of those men and women who pretended to be the salt of the earth. The Christians, as a body, were a plebeian race, and their spiritual arrogance was all the more intolerable.

And yet they gained ground in an inexplicable manner. Wherever the wealthy Greek or Jew travelled, in Asia, or Greece, or on the shores of the Mediterranean, he found adherents of the new sect quietly and firmly settled. They were often thriving people, as they attended to their own affairs, quarrelled with nobody, and wasted nothing in riotous living. They associated chiefly with one another, and had their own meetings for religious worship. But they would take no part in the religious ceremonies of paganism, and would not even eat anything which they knew to have been laid upon an idol's altar. It was useless to argue with them, or to remind them that wise men among the pagans conformed to the national religious customs, though they derided the popular belief in gods and goddesses. These obstinate people, who were mechanics, or shopkeepers, or even fishermen, accounted themselves wiser than their betters, and they deserved all the social and judicial annoyances to which they were subjected.

III. Nor did the Christians find more favour with the speculative theorists who called themselves philosophers. The stern and self-repressing follower of Zeno, the pleasure-loving disciple of Epicurus, and the thoughtful, critical Aristotelian, agreed in regarding Christianity as a mean and contemptible superstition. Such theorists were found everywhere in the chief centres of civilization. Not only in intellectual Athens and voluptuous Corinth, but in masterful Rome, and wherever the characteristic Roman intellect made itself felt, those philosophic systems had their adherents. For the Roman intelligence, enlightened by Greek culture, was now in its most energetic activity. Its literary power betrayed but few signs of decay, though the golden age of Augustus was passed. Its artistic faculty was at its highest, as was shown by the multitude of marble statues in the public buildings and private houses of Rome. The architectural gifts of the Romans were great, and they left behind them many masterpieces worthy of the conquerors of the world. They had learned from the Etrurians the use of the arch, unknown to the Greeks, as a principle of construction, suited to the vastness of their own designs, and they had invented a new order of architecture, the Composite; not, it is true, very pure or satisfying, but exhibiting their power of assimilating and combining the thoughts of other men.

Thus, in the full activity of his intellect, the Roman conqueror and colonizer often adopted some one of the philosophic systems to which the genius of Greece had given birth, and applied it to practical purposes with all his own rough and daring energy. And thus it was that the Christians of the Apostolic period constantly found themselves confronted by an enemy very unlike the coarse and vulgar mob of illiterate and unconverted Jews and Gentiles.

This enemy, too, was all the more dangerous an opponent to the progress of the gospel, because it exercised a material influence on the weaker and more superficial minds among the Christians themselves. Its attacks were for the most part not directed against the details of Christian morals, which were in many respects akin to the teachings of the Stoics and the Aristotelians. It was the elementary conception of a religion based on the humiliation of Jesus which excited the ridicule of the philosophers, and in many places bewildered the believers, even where it did not seduce them to absolute unbelief.

How this came about it is easy to understand, if we judge by our own present experience of the effects of philosophic theories in predisposing people's minds against the obvious meanings of St. Paul's writings in the New Testament. It is true that we have adopted a new phraseology of our own.

Nobody cares now for the speculative philosophies of ancient Greece. People would as soon regulate their eating of beans by the teaching of Pythagoras as deliberately modify their interpretation of the Bible by studying the Dialogues of Plato or the " Memorabilia " of Xenophon. Our present oracle calls itself science, especially physical science, or physiology—excellent subjects of knowledge in themselves, though by no means equivalent to that knowledge of God and the invisible world which Christianity unfolds. And it is only necessary to observe the widespread influence of certain scientific theories at this very day to enable us to realize the bewildering philosophic sneers upon the humble but quickly receptive members of the Church of the apostles.

Placed thus in the midst of a hostile society, the internal affairs of the apostolic Christians were in various respects singularly unlike anything we are accustomed to. Of these, one of the most important was the absence of those documents which go by the name of creeds. The simplest and earliest of these summaries of belief, known as the Apostles' Creed, was not yet in existence. The faith of the believers rested entirely on what had been taught them by the apostles themselves and their companions in the work of conversion, and it was to the enforcement and explanation of the doctrines thus originally taught, that St. Paul's and the other Epistles were mainly directed. As time went on, things changed in this respect, but during the apostolic period no one, either teacher or learner, had formed any conception of a formal dogmatic statement of Christian truths such as was drawn up nearly three centuries later at the Council of Nice. Thus, if the believers were left without any condensed summary of Christian doctrines like the Nicene Creed, still less had they any idea of such a document as that which is known as the Athanasian Creed, which is essentially of an argumentative character, discussing the doctrines of Christianity from a controversial point of view. Indeed, if we wish to realize to the full the difference between the intellectual life of the apostolic Christians and that of a later period, it is only necessary to compare St. Paul's method of teaching controversial subjects, as in the Epistles to the Romans and the Corinthians, with the method adopted by the author of the Athanasian Creed in expounding the doctrine of the Incarnation.

Nowadays, it is almost impossible to contemplate religious doctrines in the manner in which the early Christians contemplated them. We see them under the lurid light of theological controversy. No one can escape its effects. The most ignorant and uneducated are affected by the prevailing influence, for those who teach them are themselves the product of an age unlike anything that has gone before it. No matter what religious communion a man belongs to, the teachers in that communion have been made what they are by successive generations of controversy. For more educated people, it is an age of discussions, of newspapers, of magazines, and of public meetings ; an age not of enthusiasm, but of restlessness, which satisfies its feeble ardours by setting up innumerable societies and collecting subscriptions, all duly advertised in influential periodicals.

IV. Compared with this artificial religious life in which we are now involved, the method by which the apostolic Churches first learned the doctrines of Christianity was simplicity itself, and can with difficulty be understood by minds educated like our own. The believers owed all their knowledge to the occasional visits of an apostle, and rarely were personally instructed by any one else. The older believers, of course, instructed the younger ; and conversions often followed from the conversations of Christians with their unbelieving friends and neighbours. But, both in general outlines and in details, all Christian doctrine was taught by word of mouth, by St. Paul, or his companions, or one of the other apostles.

Much of this instruction was given in conversation and private intercourse ; but the chief method seems to have taken the form of addresses to gatherings of the believers, more or less numerous, corresponding to what we now call preaching, or what perhaps might be termed catechetical instruction, only that there were no such things as catechisms, or any similar convenient summaries of definite religious doctrines.

V. What was St. Paul's manner, and that of the other apostles, when they spoke to an assembly, may be understood from their manner in the Epistles. It must have been destitute of all elaborate formality; discursive in arrangement—probably with little or no arrangement at all; full of substantial thought and meaning, though, of course, not condensed into a comparatively few sentences, as is the instruction given in the Epistles; varying according to the characteristic personality of each apostle, but never for a moment degenerating into those vices of wordiness and rhetorical amplification with which modern oratory has made us so painfully familiar.

That St. Paul's preaching was wonderfully forcible, we have every reason to believe; but it is equally certain that religious doctrines were presented by him to his hearers in a more simply practical form than is now possible, when discussion and controversy have moulded Christian truths into crystallized forms of words, in which every speaker and writer has to express his own thoughts.

VI. No element, however, in the early Christian life is so strange to our eyes as the conflict, nearly universal, between the believers of Hebrew origin and those who had been brought up as Gentiles. I call it a conflict, for the word is not too strong for the feelings of exasperation and dread produced by the persistent efforts of the Jewish party to enforce the observance of the whole Mosaic law, including the rite of circumcision, upon all Gentile Christians. In our eyes the conflict has lost all practical interest, and we may be disposed to regard it as a mere quarrel, such as might be expected from an ill-educated and unspiritual generation. Any such conclusion, however, is inconsistent with a recollection of that conception of the gospel which was presented by St. Paul and the other apostles to the universal Church. Yet certainly, at first sight, the conflict was an amazing one, and the modern reader may be pardoned if he is bewildered at the recollection, that by such a dispute the peace and happiness of nearly the whole Church were disturbed, and its very existence seemingly imperilled. For the conflict raged almost everywhere. There was scarcely a city or a village where the Gentile believers were not agitated by these demands upon their credulity, for the Jews themselves seemed to be everywhere. Their national fondness for settling wherever the Roman imperial administration made it practicable had carried them to the most important cities of the empire; and as these settlements yielded many converts to Christianity, their position in the infant Church was numerically important, even when their number was not equal to that of the Gentile believers.

To the Gentile believers themselves it was scant consolation to see that the theory which harassed them was put forward by their Jewish fellow-Christians from very questionable motives. The men who tormented them might be proud and domineering; but the difficulty was, how to answer them. The Gentile Christians had been taught to venerate Moses as an inspired law-giver; and it was by appealing to the Jewish Scriptures that the claim of Jesus to be regarded as the Saviour of all men was vindicated by St. Paul and the other apostles. How, then, could they, brought up in the outer world of heathenism, pretend to set up their opinions against people who had been the special objects of Divine favour? What right had they to choose for themselves certain portions of this holy Mosaic system, and reject the rest? However steadily their common sense and secret convictions might rebel against these pretensions, however keenly they felt in their hearts that there was something radically unsound in the Judaizing theory, they could not put their convictions into logical shape, and silence their tormentors while they satisfied themselves.

Then came the great apostle, himself a converted Jew, and placed the whole case before them, first in personal intercourse, and afterwards, as time went on, in letters to different local communities where the strife had been hottest. It was unnecessary, he showed them, to enter into any minute examination of the details of the Mosaic law, or to divide it into its ritual and moral elements. It was a mistake to imagine that men's obligations towards

God and towards one another depended upon the ten commandments or any teaching of Moses. These obligations always existed, and the object of the Mosaic system was to serve as a schoolmaster to bring mankind to Christ, by showing them that it is impossible to serve God by our own unaided strength. Every one who tries to keep the law of God, and thus place himself in the position of one who makes a bargain with his Maker, utterly fails. Thus man learns the extremely difficult lesson of his own helplessness, and comes to God in humility and faith, asking for salvation from his sins as a free gift. This God gives him in that spiritual presence of the Holy Ghost, which it was the object of the humiliation and death of Christ to procure. Thus the moral law is not abolished, but fulfilled, and the whole Mosaic law, as such, disappears from among divinely constituted authorities.

Against this reasoning the Judaizing party could make no head. Their influence seems to have died away, and the whole Church, no longer torn by internal dissensions, was able to prepare in peace for a life and death struggle with the ferocity of Roman paganism. While Christianity had been winning its triumphs in the chief seats of Græco-Roman cultivation, a specially brutalizing influence had been steadily at work among the populace of the largest and most thickly inhabited cities of the empire. The whole population, indeed, was in process of deterioration, from the imperial court downwards. Scarcely a trace was left of the old public spirit of the republic which had fought against Hannibal, and against the hordes of northern barbarians.

VII. The general building of amphitheatres in the chief cities of Italy was at once a cause and an effect of this growth of national brutality. The Coliseum at Rome, and the amphitheatre at Verona show us how large were the sums expended on such structures, and how popular were the exhibitions for which they were designed. There the hired gladiators fought with one another; while a more debasing practice can scarcely be conceived than that which authorized the excited multitude to determine, by a movement of their thumbs, whether a vanquished and prostrate combatant should be spared or instantly slaughtered by the victor in the fight.

Thus was nourished in the populace that hideous passion for the sight of blood and mortal suffering which lies deep in the human heart, when degraded to its lowest level, and thus was the Roman mob prepared to delight in the horrible enjoyment provided for them by the Emperor Nero, when that grotesque and licentious tyrant cast upon the Christians the odium of setting fire to the city, in order to turn away popular suspicion from himself.

Then came the deadly conflict, and the Christians were found faithful. Day after day they heard the cry of the bloodthirsty populace, "Christianos ad leones!" More appalling than the sword of the gladiator was the rush of the savage lions, reserved for such shows, that they might tear the limbs of the faithful followers of Him who died upon the cross; and when each tragedy was over in the bloodstained arena, the gratified multitude and their rulers went back to their homes, eager for more and more slaughter, and imagining that the cause for which the martyrs died was for ever crushed out.

The same generation witnessed the final extinction of the Jewish nation as a people claiming a national independence. History tells us of no resistance to an overwhelming force more heroic than that of the Jews to their imperial conqueror. The story of the sieges of Jotapata and Jerusalem, in all their terrible details, places in the clearest light not merely the horrors of all war, but the hereditary tenacity of the Jewish race, and the force of the iron hand of Rome, when it was stretched out to destroy those whom it could not control.

Only one power could ever withstand that iron hand, and that power was more than human. It was the Church of the poor and humble, whose early history, as it spread itself throughout the provinces of the empire, I have attempted to sketch, conscious at once of the greatness of the theme and the feebleness with which my words have responded to its inspiring power.

At the same time, the picture which I have here

drawn, however faint its outlines, may be of use to those of my readers who may be disposed to re-examine the New Testament Epistles for themselves, as a record of the life of the first century. The intellect must be dull, and the sympathies cold indeed, which are not moved by such a study, and transported from the dreary troubles of to-day to a time when saints and apostles were living in the world, and men and women died for Christ, instead of disputing about Him.

If such a study of the Epistles appears attractive before it is undertaken, its prosecution has a charm which must be felt to be understood. And who is there amongst us who would not be the happier for being enabled thus to realize a little better all the truths that are implied in the doctrine of the Communion of Saints? Even those—how few they are!—who have nearly completed their lives without being bruised and wounded in the struggle with doubts and temptations, cannot altogether escape the paralyzing influence of those strange complications of good and evil, of knowledge and ignorance, of sincerity and worldliness, which mark the age in which our lot is cast.

For every one, then, who is not hopelessly indifferent or prosaic, it is no small gain to be able to live over again, in thought, the days long gone by. For after all, in the things that concern eternity, a thousand years are as one day; and the records of the life of the apostles and those who knew them are like the story of what happened among our own friends and kindred only yesterday.

VIII. On some questions, indeed, which are of no little interest to-day, the apostolic Epistles yield little or no information. On the general organization of the Christian Churches, or what is commonly called Church government, we have to content ourselves with noticing a few isolated facts; important in the way of suggestion, but that is all. Over the communities to which St. Paul writes he exercises absolute authority; occasionally giving minute and detailed directions on practical matters, and taking it for granted that no one would dispute his right to be obeyed.

From the Epistles to Timothy and Titus, it is evident that the control of the affairs of each town or district was vested in the hands of a single person. To Timothy and Titus, as being charged respectively with the control of the Churches in Ephesus and Crete, St. Paul gives directions for the appointment of these local chiefs or bishops, specifying carefully the qualifications necessary for the office. Similar qualifications are specified for the subordinate office of deacon, apparently the same as that which is spoken of by St. Peter under the term elder, when he calls himself an elder, and exhorts the elders generally to piety and zeal.

Of the rules by which the Christians conducted their assemblies the Epistles give scarcely any indications. In writing to Timothy, St. Paul directs that supplications, prayers, intercessions, and thanksgivings should be offered for all men; and in particular he names kings and persons in authority, in order that every one might lead a quiet and peaceable life. In writing to the Corinthians, he reproves them for certain scandalous excesses in the celebration of the Lord's Supper, one effect of which was to make the poor man ashamed of his poverty. St. James's reproof to the believers for the same subservience to rich people in their assemblies shows the strength of the abuse condemned, but gives no information on the character of the religious services of the time.

On one subject of great practical importance, the silence of the Epistles is conclusive as to the instruction which the apostles gave to the infant Churches. Not a word is said as to the attempt made by the believers at Jerusalem to share their property with one another, as recorded in the Acts of the Apostles.* It is clear that the attempt practically failed; though it was a natural and praiseworthy effect of their newly learnt feelings of universal brotherhood. The believers speedily found that human feelings were too strong for abstract theory; and that then, as now, not socialism, but individualism, was the only possible basis of a healthy Christian life.

Such questions as these, however, may be set aside, as of secondary importance, by the reader who would enjoy the full benefit of the invigorating

* Acts ii. 44, 45.

influence of the historical study of the New Testament Epistles. The historical spirit, being essentially calm and unprejudiced, seeks for real information only, and examines with judicial acuteness such testimony as is accessible to the persevering inquirer. And it is a grave mistake to imagine that this calmness of judgment is incompatible with a deep sense of the importance of the subject under investigation. The very contrary is the case. The more momentous are the issues involved, the more dispassionate ought to be our investigations as to actual facts, and the more constant our fear of inventing conclusions which the real facts do not warrant. Only those readers who study the Epistles in this strictly historical spirit can yield themselves up to the fascination of the conclusions at which they arrive when they find themselves in the living presence of their brothers and sisters in the faith, who lived and died for Christ eighteen hundred years ago.

Then, indeed, we may forget the present in our sympathy with the past. We may realize in our own case the three great truths which animated the followers of Christ in the old days. We may live in thought among them, and hear how they talked to one another of the marvellous and inscrutable election of God, which had made them possessors of the Holy Ghost,* and taught them to look forward to the return of Jesus to this world in His glory, when they would once more be united to those whom they

* See chapters xix., xx., xxi.

had loved and lost. This is the reward that may be expected by every honest Christian mind that is wearied with this strange, unsatisfying life, and turns, as the tired traveller drinks from the cool springs in the hot desert, to the recollection of those who are gone before.

CHAPTER XIX.

THE MILLENNIUM.

In the foregoing chapters it has been taken for granted that the reader is already acquainted with the theological and philosophical subjects of which mention has been made in connection with the details of St. Paul's Epistles and those of his brother apostles. There are, however, a few subjects which still give rise to so much controversy, and involve principles of so wide a range, that they require a somewhat fuller treatment than was convenient when our attention was first called to them.

Such is the doctrine of the Millennium, or personal reign of Christ upon earth. That St. Paul and the other apostles taught the Christians of their day to look forward to the personal coming of Christ, and not simply to expect to see Him in another life, is as undeniable as that they taught them to believe in an eternal future of happiness; but the prophecies which have given rise to expectations concerning the events which are to follow upon earth after the return of Christ are not touched upon in the apostolic Epistles.

In almost all ages of the Church many persons have held that these prophecies show that Christ will reign, with His saints, here on earth, for a thousand years; after which will come the second, or general resurrection. Hence those who hold these views are popularly termed Millenarians, or Chiliasts, according to the corresponding Greek numeral. From the Patristic period till to-day, there have been two schools of opinion on the question, represented by Lactantius and Jerome among the Fathers. One of these schools holds that during the Millennium Christ will reign at Jerusalem; and that the Jewish race, at length converted to a belief in Him as the true Messiah, will be restored to their ancient home. The other school attributes to the prophecies in question a spiritual meaning only, and sees in them a forecast of the practical devotion to the glorified Jesus which will distinguish all nations during the thousand years' reign.

Both of these interpretations have attractions for many minds; for it is the case, that the more obscure a prophecy is, the greater is the eagerness of some persons to undertake its interpretation, and the more positive they are that their own interpretation is correct. It is well if they do not accuse of stupidity or perverseness all who cannot see with their eyes and hear with their ears.

But whatever is the correct interpretation of the prophecies in question, it is important to remember that they have no bearing upon our knowledge of the life of the apostolic Church, as unfolded to us in the apostolic Epistles. Whatever St. Paul and his brother apostles knew or believed respecting the details of the life that would follow upon earth after the return of Christ, they did not communicate their knowledge to those to whom they wrote their letters.

And I am the more anxious to call attention to the fact, because, with the great majority of devout minds, any suspicion that a cordial acceptance of St. Paul's teaching necessarily leads to a belief in Millenarianism, prevents them from deriving from it that practical guidance which it is calculated to afford. The result of a sympathetic study of the life of the apostolic Church is not only, as I have already pointed out, to enlarge our knowledge of Christianity, and of the fortunes of humanity, but to quicken our perception of the profound reality of the doctrine of the Communion of Saints. Especially it has that influence upon those of us whose lives are darkened by the deaths of those with whose lives everything that brightened existence was bound up. With such persons the one question which they are always asking themselves is this: How and when shall we see again those who are gone? And when we recall the faith of the oldest days of the Church, a new light brightens the gloom of this world. We linger in the churchyards where lie the remains of those who are gone from our sight, and as each sculptured cross or simple memorial kindles afresh our thoughts of the relics, ever sacred to us, which are hidden below, faith sees the heavens opened, and One, fairer than the children of men, returning to the scene of His sorrows. And then the graves give up their dead, and we look upon the loved features once more; the sweet voices speak again; and while we wait and watch, they are already with Jesus. Then comes our own turn. We know not how it comes about, but so it is. The long-looked-for moment has arrived. We are with those whom we loved, and there is to be no separation for ever. Love is to be thenceforth the source of joy only, as it has hitherto been the source of more pain than happiness; and whatever is to be the destiny of this visible world, we and the recovered lost ones are *together* with the Lord.

But will all this take place in our lifetime? it is naturally asked. More than eighteen hundred years have gone by since St. Paul wrote to the Thessalonians that with hopes like these they should comfort one another under the loss of those who were dear to them, and yet Christ has not come. Was St. Paul, then, mistaken? That he himself believed that Christ might return during his own lifetime is certain. But what are we to think, now that all these ages have gone by, and human society has passed through stage after stage of development and growth? How can we regard the belief in the second coming as a thing affecting our practical actions? Is it not all a kind of beautiful dream, which wise men will do well to set aside, while they occupy themselves solely with the realities of death and judgment?

The reply to these natural questions is twofold. In the first place, it is, of course, a matter of choice for a good Christian whether or not he will occupy himself with the thought of the visible return of our Lord to this earth. But this I will say, that no person can study the life of the apostolic Church under the guidance of the apostolic Epistles, with an honest desire to identify himself with that life as a practical reality, and yet regard this expectation of our Lord's return as merely a subject of interesting speculation. Persons who thus regard it are out of sympathy with their fellow-Christians of the old days in a matter which affected the whole tone of their daily lives. They may think themselves more sensible and more enlightened by modern ideas than those who share the faith and feelings of ancient times in all their enthusiastic warmth, but I repeat that they are Christians of a modernized type; and that the Thessalonians and other ancient Christians would have accounted them very foolish, for all their cautious criticisms.

In the second place, St. Paul and his brother apostles invariably regarded the precise date of the second advent as a thing which God had not made known, and consequently, as furnishing no reason for our ceasing to look for it, however long delayed.

St. Paul and St. Peter themselves emphatically taught that whenever Christ should really return His coming would be unexpected, for He would come "as a thief in the night"—a phrase which makes it clear that, however obscure and enigmatical are the warnings which St. Paul gave concerning the previous manifestation of the great mystery of iniquity, they were not designed to induce us to relax for a single day our expectation that Christ might be personally amongst us. The notion that such an expectation cannot reasonably be a matter of practical importance at the present day, would have seemed absolutely absurd to the great apostle of the Gentiles. When he himself, in one of his last letters, exchanges his old expressions of expectation of Christ's coming for a simple statement that he had a desire to depart and to be with Christ, it is not because he was weary of waiting for Christ to come; it was not that "hope deferred, which maketh the heart sick," that made him anxious for death. He was worn out with his long and exhausting labours for the good of other men; and the wonder is that he was not utterly worn out long before.

The obscurity, again, of St. Paul's description of the manifestation of the power of evil, which is to precede the return of Christ, supplies no valid reason for setting aside the thought of His possible return in our own day. The obscurity is, indeed, very great; and it is deepened by the highly figurative character of the terms employed by St. Paul to convey his meaning to the Thessalonians. How far, in truth, he intended that they should understand the full meaning of his words, may be a matter of doubt. It is very possible that, as in the case of prophetic declarations in Scripture generally, this prophecy was designed only to be thoroughly understood after its accomplishment.

In the mean time, it is precisely one of those which have a special attraction for minds which delight in interpreting the enigmatical, and in converting prophecies into weapons for discomfiting a controversial adversary. St. Paul says that a mystery of iniquity is to be revealed, and that it was already at work, but was hindered in its anti-Christian triumphs by a certain opposing power, of which no definite description is given, while its ultimate disappearance from the struggle is distinctly foretold. This mystery of iniquity is termed the man of sin, who will exalt himself above all that is called God, or is worshipped; even claiming to be himself worshipped in the temple of God. As to the exact date when this man of sin will attain the climax of his atheistic power, St. Paul says nothing; but he declares that when this climax is reached, it will be accompanied by the falling away of many persons.

This man of sin will also work many signs and wonders, with the object of leading minds astray, until he himself is at last swept away by the Divine vengeance. The whole picture is at once so full of details, so strange and so suggestive, that while it stimulates to the utmost our desire to know in what degree it is applicable to real persons and events in our own time, it leaves us in the dark when we attempt any thorough and dispassionate investigation of its meaning. St. Paul's words imply that the Thessalonians knew something of the character of the power which at that time hindered the full operation of the deceiving influences of the godless mystery; but that is all that can be gathered from his brief words in the way of reliable guidance towards the solution of the difficulty.

As to any complete and candid interpretation of the whole prophecy, it appears to be impossible, until the course of human events has unfolded itself, aud new light is thrown upon the facts of history, past and present. No interpretation that I have ever heard of, or that I can invent for myself, corresponds to the complete picture drawn by St. Paul, and to the circumstances of human life, when examined without prejudice or passion. I have found no key which even seems likely to unlock the secret, and I therefore accept the simple repeated expressions in the Epistles which speak of the coming of Christ, in their practical bearing, without attempting anything more, confident that when the time comes, all will in a moment be clear.

The whole difficulty in connection with the second advent is, in truth, in harmony with the ascertained facts of human experience, whether in connection with the Christian Scriptures, or independent of them. It seems almost a truism to say that no one understands anything till some subsequently discovered fact reveals the interpretation of the past. Yet all practical action would be impossible, if we waited to understand any physical or intellectual law before taking any steps which seem to imply that we understand it. And thus, while a scriptural prophecy is a sufficient guide to practical action, it may remain obscure until light is thrown upon it by that practical action itself.

Such is the course which St. Paul recommends to the Thessalonians, and to the believers in general. Do not speculate, he says in substance, but believe. Expect the Lord to come at any time. His coming will be preceded by lying wonders; be, therefore, always prepared for them also. But remember that with God a thousand years are as one day, and one day as a thousand years. It is for man to believe and to obey; and for God to understand and to explain, only always in His own good time. Yet to us it is permitted to pray constantly, "Thy kingdom come; even so, Lord Jesus, come quickly."

CHAPTER XX.

PREDESTINATION AND FREE-WILL.

It is impossible to examine the apostolical Epistles with careful and unprejudicial attention, and yet pass over these repeated references to the doctrine of predestination and election. And it is therefore equally impossible to find ourselves in sympathy with the apostolic Church in the tone of its daily life, as long as we regard this doctrine with a half-hesitating fear or dislike, or take refuge in an arbitrary interpretation of the expressions used by St. Paul and his brother apostles. It would be an intelligible course to close our eyes altogether to the subject, as being too difficult for an ordinary man's understanding—this, I say, would be intelligible, and quite consistent with a humble faith and a reasonable performance of daily duties.

But such a course is not recommended for general adoption by the writers of the Epistles themselves. They unanimously refer to this doctrine as an elementary part of a Christian's belief, and are unconscious of its unsuitableness for ordinary understandings. The grave and even appalling aspect which it assumes in the minds of many devout persons to-day, was certainly not present to the judgment of St. Paul and the other early teachers of the gospel. And we must therefore conclude that we are mistaken, when we turn away from the subject as unpractical, or as fit for investigation only by intellects of unusual subtlety and logical power.

In recommending the honest and courageous adoption of the apostolic teaching to the general reader, I should at once admit that as a matter of mere intellectual speculation the whole subject is, without doubt, unsuited to the capacities of ordinary persons. It leads directly into those profoundly difficult metaphysical inquiries which are, for obvious reasons, as unprofitable as inquiries into the nature of the forces by which the earth and the heavens were brought into their present condition. For ordinary thinkers to attempt the solution of the old difficulty concerning the relation between "liberty" and "necessity" (to use the ancient philosophical phraseology), would be about as fruitless as the attempt to prove to a non-mathematical mind that there cannot by any possibility be such a thing as the square root of a negative quantity. What ordinary persons have a right to ask for is some such statement of the facts involved in the predestinarian doctrine as shall convince them that it is not a paralyzing doctrine, destroying all vitality in daily life, and leading to sin rather than to holiness.

The question, then, as treated by St. Paul, is to a great extent one which rests upon the ascertained phenomena of human action. And we have a most significant illustration of the practical influences of predestinarianism ready to our hand in the races which have adopted the Mohammedan creed. The belief in predestinarianism is a vigorous reality in these races; and it is certain that, so far from paralyzing their energies and seducing them into a listless inactivity, it stimulates them to unceasing efforts to obtain the ends which they desire, and which they hold to be predestinated. These ends may be unlike everything that Christianity bids men seek for, and the morality of Mohammedanism is in many respects flagrantly unchristian. But the fact remains the same as to the influence of the predestinarian belief upon the active energies of human nature. It actually impels the Mohammedan fatalist to incessant activity in the accomplishment of those ends which he holds to be already determined by Divine decrees. Whether or not he is philosophically consistent in what he does and what he thinks, it is not necessary to decide. His human nature impels him to act as he does act; and he thus serves as an example to encourage the timid Christian conscience, which fears the demoralizing effects of a belief in the supremacy of the Divine decrees upon a devout man's obedience to the laws of the gospel.

What, then, is the difficulty which serious and reasonable thinkers have a right to ask me to solve? In laying before them what appears to me to be a perfectly satisfactory practical reply, without understatement or over-statement, I must first beg their attention to a preliminary truth of the utmost moment. It will be seen, as we proceed, that the real question to be decided is this: *Can* God create a free agent? Inasmuch as the nature of the created being is in every respect the result of His own omnipotent Will, can that being be called, in any sense of the word, free?

This being the root of the difficulty, it is necessary to remind the inquirer that unless we proceed with the utmost caution we shall find ourselves attempting to solve a problem which, from the nature of the case, is entirely beyond the reach of the human intellect, and which, therefore, no man in his senses would attempt to solve. That problem is, *How* does God produce those effects of which His Will is the sole and the efficient cause? In other words, what is the *mode* in which God acts, as the cause of everything that takes place in the universe? Now, it is obvious that in order to understand this essential nature of the Divine operations the created intellect must cease to be a created intellect, and must possess in itself that creating power which belongs only to One who is eternal as well as omnipotent. To comprehend *how* God acts, a man must *be* God, for he is destitute of any experience of his own, to guide him in penetrating into the mystery which he would explain.

Our own experience, when we reflect upon it, supplies no clue to guide us in a region beyond its limits. We accomplish our ends by what we call some sort of process or instrumentality. We can do nothing without forming a plan, or intention, which we then take steps to put into execution. If I desire simply to lift my foot from the ground, I first form the intention to do this; then, by means of my brain, I put in motion certain nerves, which communicate an activity to the tendons of my leg; and thus, still by means of nerves, I move my foot.

But with God nothing of the kind is necessary. This we know and understand. We understand our own methods of accomplishing our purposes; and at the same time we are certain that no such methods can be attributed to God. But here we are compelled to stop. Our knowledge of God's method of producing results is purely negative. All we know of it is that it is not ours. We know that, as a matter of fact, such and such effects have been produced by Him, and that is all.

It is undeniable, then, that the utmost caution is necessary in deciding that God cannot have accomplished any particular end, on the ground that it was beyond the reach of His power. It is not true that it would be absurd to say that there is literally nothing which is beyond the power of an omnipotent and eternal Being. God could not create another

God, omnipotent and eternal like Himself, and in all respects His own equal. This truth is included in our elementary idea of God, and therefore must be accepted without fear of error.

In discussing the doctrine of free-will and predestination, we are concerned with a very different class of ideas. If there is predestination, it is argued, there *can be* no freedom of action, and consequently, no moral responsibility. This, however, is only another way of stating the assertion that there can be no freedom of action in any created being. The Creator knows beforehand the exact nature of all the powers, moral and intellectual, of the creature whom He forms. He knows how that creature will be influenced by the combined operation of these qualities, or gifts, with which the created being is endowed; He knows what the result of this combination of feelings, or motives, will be, in every possible variety of circumstances. He thus foresees what will be the course pursued by this being through all time, even down to the most trivial thoughts and events of daily life. This is that Divine foreknowledge of which St. Paul speaks in writing to the Romans; and the reality of this foreknowledge no rational person can deny.

Further, inasmuch as these intellectual and moral elements in our nature were given to each of us by our Creator, their combined operations are really the result of His will; and therefore, it is argued, we cannot be blamed for our thoughts and actions, any more than for the shape of our features or the constitution of our bodies.

This, then, is the practical question. When God creates each one of us, does He endow us with a certain power of choice between conflicting inclinations? or are we so helpless that our actual conduct is determined by the strength of the inclination which at the moment is most powerful within us? Analyzing our mental processes still further, is, or is not, our final decision the result of the entrance of a third motive, essentially moral in its quality, which decides between the claims of the already conflicting inclinations, and is, in other words, our free-will? This, then, is *the* question; and I repeat, that it cannot be determined by any antecedent speculations as to what is, or is not, in the power of God to accomplish. It is simply a question of fact, to be determined by our personal experience, and that of the rest of mankind.

And surely the universal consent of mankind is decisive in the matter. Can it be seriously argued that the whole human race is under a delusion, when it recognizes in every person a real power of choice in the daily affairs of human life? I do not pretend to say how far this power of choice extends, but I say that it exists, and that every one is so certain of its existence in himself, that he admits that he can be praised or blamed without being the victim of injustice, according to his actual conduct. The whole world is agreed in repudiating the notion that men and women are helpless machines. From the private intercourse of individual men, up to the combined actions of states and nations, we are all agreed in holding that our power of choice is not a phantom, but so undeniable a reality that no one complains of being treated as a free agent.

Every one, indeed, complains if no limits are set to this system of rewards and punishments. Every one complains if he is punished for yielding to irresistible temptations. But the very complaint itself assumes that there are some temptations which are not irresistible—that is, which a man is able to resist if he chooses, or, in other words, if he exerts his power as a free agent.

If, then, we know that we are capable of acting as free agents in our dealings with one another, we are capable of the same freedom of choice in connection with our own duties towards God; for the question is not whether we are really free, under all possible circumstances, but whether we *can be* free under any. And on this point we are all agreed in action, whatever the lovers of metaphysical puzzles may allege in the way of abstract theory.

The conclusion of the whole matter is, therefore, as follows. All things are predestinated, and yet we are free agents, because we are predestinated to be free agents. The two doctrines may seem to contradict one another, but this is only because our intellect is limited, and does not enable us to understand the manner in which the Creator accomplishes

His Will. We know, in other words, that predestination *must be* true; and we know that the doctrine of free-will *is* true.

Other considerations, indeed, have to be taken into account, if we would find ourselves in complete sympathy with the thoughts and feelings of the apostolic Christians. They held not only that all things are the result of the sovereign Will of God, but that every believer was under the special influence of the Spirit of God, given to him in order that he might be conformed to the image of God in Jesus Christ; and that, being thus predestinated to this conformity, all things worked together for his good. That this conviction was as consolatory as it was profound, will not be doubted; and we may be sure that it exercised a permanent and powerful influence in enabling the faithful to undergo the special trials of the time, ending so often in actual martyrdom. They cheerfully bore the troubles of daily life, as being a predestinated element in the process by which they were made obedient to the Divine Will; and when martyrdom came, still it was the result of the same predestinating sovereignty. And therefore, instead of bewildering themselves with metaphysical subtleties, they obeyed the Will of God, whether in life or in death. Such was the influence of predestinarianism, when all Christians were predestinarians.

CHAPTER XXI.

MODERN OBJECTIONS TO A BELIEF IN MIRACLES.

THE critical reader of St. Paul's Epistles is sometimes unable to identify himself with the life of the first Christians, because he is haunted with a suspicion that the miraculous events to which the apostle refers did not really take place as actual matters of fact.

Modern ingenuity, indeed, has devised a very summary method for disposing of such statements when they occur in narratives like the four Gospels, or the Acts of the Apostles. What is called the mythical theory is applied without hesitation to those statements; and we are asked to believe that because certain wonderful stories, purely fabulous, were gradually crystallized into historical realities by the votaries of heathen religions, therefore all accounts of supernatural incidents are to be set down as the result of a similar process of transformation. The audacity with which the German Professor Strauss carried this theory into the whole life of our Lord startled so many people with its novelty, that for a time "The Life of Jesus" acquired a notoriety and exerted an influence which have now passed away. Logic, even with the headlong British thinker, has resumed its sway, and critics of the New Testament have come to see that the element of supernaturalism in the Christian Scriptures cannot be got rid of by attributing it to that superstitious tendency in human nature which converted the shadowy fables of uncivilized Greece into the concrete gods and goddesses who figure in the "Iliad" and the "Odyssey."

In dealing with the supernatural element in St. Paul's writings, a totally different method for discrediting it has been adopted, and has found favour with many persons of undoubted intelligence and sincerity. This view may be briefly described as the molecular difficulty. It is held that everything that exists, and which is not strictly non-corporeal, is made up of a multitude of extraordinarily small particles, called atoms. These, when combined into groups, are called molecules; and it is by the varying combinations and movements of these molecules that every alteration in the condition of our bodies, and in that of the earth, and all things upon it, is effected. Inasmuch as it is by means of our brain that we think and feel, and our brain is made up of molecules, all our actions are dependent upon some sort of molecular movements and combinations.

From this it follows that, as every corporeal act or change is the result of some movement or change in many molecules, which again are connected with many others, no limit can be set to the modifications in the physical system of the universe which result from the introduction of each successive cause of movement in its constituent elements. Each successive phenomenon is the result of some previous molecular activity; and all this vast system of life and death, of health and disease, of growth and decay, in the midst of which we live, is carried on in accordance with certain fixed rules, which are termed the laws of nature, so that nothing which contravenes these laws can possibly take place.

A miracle, on the other hand, is a contravention of these laws. Those who maintain that any supernatural event has taken place, assert that some change has been effected in the molecular condition of a human body, or in that of the earth and its surroundings, without the agency of any previously existing molecular movements or combinations. As there is no limit to the extent to which the effect of these changes may extend, the whole system of the universe is thus thrown out of gear—a result which, it is alleged, is simply incredible.

In reply to this difficulty, I admit at once, that such a disturbance must undoubtedly take place, supposing that the molecular theory of the universe is sound. Its soundness I neither affirm nor dispute; but, granting its soundness, I would point out to those who disbelieve in miracles, that the molecular condition of the universe is incessantly modified by the voluntary agency of man. It is by our choice and interference that the operation of the laws of nature is, in innumerable instances, carried out. However vast is the field in which these laws produce their results without the agency of man, he does, as a matter of fact, habitually interfere in the action of natural law, and become an agent in the entire system of the universe.

Thus, various diseased conditions of our bodies are cured by the action of certain known remedies. In other words, the molecular condition of our bodies is modified by the instrumentality of certain visible substances, which themselves undergo certain fixed molecular changes in producing the anticipated result. But it is the will of man that first begins these particular operations of medicinal substances. The medicines do not manufacture themselves, or administer themselves. Man manufactures them, and man administers them, and is thus the real originator of the molecular changes which they involve.

The corn grows in the fields, and ripens under the action of the sun and the rain; and men and cattle are fed, and the routine of agricultural life is carried on in harmony with ascertained physiological and chemical laws; but it is the voluntary agency of man that begins the work of growth, and sets the causes at work which produce the wonderful result. He cannot, it is true, change the direction of the wind at his pleasure, or institute alternations of sunshine and showers to suit the various crops that he is cultivating; but he can actually change the climate in which they grow. He can plant or cut down trees on a large scale, and alter the whole atmospheric state of a district from dryness to moisture, or from moisture to dryness. Still, I say, it is man who is practically the agent who causes these boundless molecular modifications in a portion of the universe.

In the case of a miracle, these same modifications are effected without the operation of those previous physical causes which man is obliged to set in motion, in order to produce the effects which he desires. But in each case it is the power of God that really produces the result. When man sows the seed in the ground, it does not germinate of itself. The molecular particles, by whose recombinations the seed throws out its roots and buds and leaves, do not move or affect one another by any inherent powers of their own. God, who alone has life in Himself, works these changes by His ever-present power, following certain exact stages, which He has laid down for Himself to observe, and which we call the laws of nature. For a law is not a force; it is a rule, and has no effect unless it is enforced by an actually existing being. We are the victims of a species of verbal sleight-of-hand when we speak of law, which is an abstraction, as if it were a concrete reality. The operation of the remedies that we take for the cure of diseases is, in like manner, due to the Divine agency, which carries out in each case those molecular combinations which produce the healing of the diseased portions of our bodies. The direct agency of God Himself never ceases or is suspended; and it extends from the movements of the microscopic animalcules which elude the vision of our unassisted eyesight, to the regions where suns and solar systems are so distant that even to the eye that looks at them through the most far-reaching telescope, they seem only bright specks of light in the boundless firmament of heaven.

When, then, at the intercession of a man, God works what is called a miracle, He is simply doing, in answer to prayer, what he is incessantly doing in compliance with certain acts of ours, in which the initiative is taken by ourselves. The difference of the two cases lies in the frequency of their occurrence. Human life is carried on through the constant enforcement by God of the rules of the physical universe, while in the case of miracles, which if they were not rare would cease to be miracles, the action of the ordinary physical laws is varied in some manner not in harmony with their ordinary operation. But in both cases the only real author of the molecular changes that take place is God Himself; and in both cases the voluntary agency of man enters in, and seems to set in motion the agency of omnipotence.

In reality, all things, both natural and supernatural, are illustrations of the Divine Will. And therefore, when we examine the evidences alleged for any reputed miracle, we do this without any suspicion that it cannot have taken place, because it must have involved an extensive interference with the normal condition of the universe, and produced consequences far beyond its own limits. We see such interferences incessantly going on, and think nothing of them. If we only lift up our hand or utter a few words, alterations are produced in the molecular combinations of the atmosphere which spread far and wide, we know not where. Being familiar with such phenomena, we think nothing of them, and classify them under the general heading of the laws of nature. But the phenomenon are not thus explained, or even analyzed, as long as we overlook the elementary phenomena of our own will, which must be taken into account in any really scientific classification of the facts of cause and effect which come under our personal experience.

Remembering all this, we approach the proofs that may be offered of the occurrence of any miracle, ancient or modern, just as we test the evidence of any extraordinary occurrence in which no question of the supernatural is concerned. We are told, for instance, that some person has lived to be a hundred years old. We know that this is in a high degree improbable, but it is not impossible; and if we have to inquire into the fact, we exercise the utmost caution in sifting the evidence laid before us. Just so when a miracle is reported, whether of the first or the nineteenth century. All probability is against it; but for all that it may be true, and, if true, it is simply one of the unusual exercises of the power of Him in whom we live, and move, and have our being. It is a question of fact, and nothing more. And the explanation of the fact is to be found in the recognition of the presence and power of Him Who inhabits eternity, and Who has foreseen and foreordained all things that exist, from the foundation of the world.

THE END.

PRINTED BY WILLIAM CLOWES AND SONS, LIMITED, LONDON AND BECCLES.

A LIST OF

KEGAN PAUL, TRENCH, & PUBLICATIONS.

1 *Paternoster Square,*
London.

A LIST OF
KEGAN PAUL, TRENCH, & CO.'S PUBLICATIONS.

CONTENTS.

	PAGE		PAGE
GENERAL LITERATURE	2	MILITARY WORKS	28
PARCHMENT LIBRARY	17	POETRY	28
PULPIT COMMENTARY	19	WORKS OF FICTION	33
INTERNATIONAL SCIENTIFIC SERIES	26	BOOKS FOR THE YOUNG	34

A. K. H. B.—FROM A QUIET PLACE. A New Volume of Sermons. Crown 8vo. 5s.

ALLEN (Rev. R.) M.A.—ABRAHAM; HIS LIFE, TIMES, AND TRAVELS, 3,800 years ago. With Map. Second Edition. Post 8vo. 6s.

ALLIES (T. W.) M.A.—PER CRUCEM AD LUCEM. The Result of a Life. 2 vols. Demy 8vo. 25s.

A LIFE'S DECISION. Crown 8vo. 7s. 6d.

ALLNATT (F. J. B.) B.D.—THE WITNESS OF ST. MATTHEW. An Inquiry into the Sequence of Inspired Thought pervading the First Gospel, and into its Result of Unity, Symmetry, and Completeness, as a Perfect Portrait of the Perfect Man. Crown 8vo. 5s.

AMOS (Prof. Sheldon)—THE HISTORY AND PRINCIPLES OF THE CIVIL LAW OF ROME. An aid to the study of Scientific and Comparative Jurisprudence. Demy 8vo. 16s.

ANCIENT and MODERN BRITONS: a Retrospect. 2 vols. demy 8vo. 24s.

ANDERDON (Rev. W. H.)—FASTI APOSTOLICI. A Chronology of the Years between the Ascension of Our Lord and the Martyrdom of SS. Peter and Paul. Second Edition Enlarged. Square 8vo. 5s.

EVENINGS WITH THE SAINTS. Crown 8vo. 5s.

ANDERSON (David)—'SCENES' IN THE COMMONS. Crown 8vo. 5s.

ARMSTRONG (Richard A.) B.A.— LATTER-DAY TEACHERS. Six Lectures. Small crown 8vo. 2s. 6d.

AUBERTIN (J. J.)—A FLIGHT TO MEXICO. With 7 full-page Illustrations and a Railway Map of Mexico. Crown 8vo. 7s. 6d.

BADGER (George Percy) D.C.L.—AN ENGLISH-ARABIC LEXICON. In which the equivalents for English Words and Idiomatic Sentences are rendered into literary and colloquial Arabic. Royal 4to. 80s.

Kegan Paul, Trench, & Co.'s Publications. 3

BAGEHOT (*Walter*)—THE ENGLISH CONSTITUTION. New and Revised Edition. Crown 8vo. 7s. 6d.
LOMBARD STREET. A Description of the Money Market. Eighth Edition. Crown 8vo. 7s. 6d.
ESSAYS ON PARLIAMENTARY REFORM. Crown 8vo. 5s.
SOME ARTICLES ON THE DEPRECIATION OF SILVER, AND TOPICS CONNECTED WITH IT. Demy 8vo. 5s.

BAGENAL (*Philip H.*)—THE AMERICAN-IRISH AND THEIR INFLUENCE ON IRISH POLITICS. Crown 8vo. 5s.

BAGOT (*Alan*) *C.E.*—ACCIDENTS IN MINES : Their Causes and Prevention. Crown 8vo. 6s.
THE PRINCIPLES OF COLLIERY VENTILATION. Second Edition, greatly enlarged, crown 8vo. 5s.
THE PRINCIPLES OF CIVIL ENGINEERING IN ESTATE MANAGEMENT. Crown 8vo. 7s. 6d.

BAKER (*Sir Sherston, Bart.*)—THE LAWS RELATING TO QUARANTINE. Crown 8vo. 12s. 6d.

BALDWIN (*Capt. J. H.*)—THE LARGE AND SMALL GAME OF BENGAL AND THE NORTH-WESTERN PROVINCES OF INDIA. Small 4to. With 20 Illustrations. New and Cheaper Edition. Small 4to. 10s. 6d.

BALLIN (*Ada S. and F. L.*)—A HEBREW GRAMMAR. With Exercises selected from the Bible. Crown 8vo. 7s. 6d.

BARCLAY (*Edgar*)—MOUNTAIN LIFE IN ALGERIA. Crown 4to. With numerous Illustrations by Photogravure. 16s.

BARLOW (*J. W.*) *M.A.*—THE ULTIMATUM OF PESSIMISM. An Ethical Study. Demy 8vo. 6s.

BARNES (*William*)—OUTLINES OF REDECRAFT (LOGIC). With English Wording. Crown 8vo. 3s.

BAUR (*Ferdinand*) *Dr. Ph., Professor in Maulbronn.*—A PHILOLOGICAL INTRODUCTION TO GREEK AND LATIN FOR STUDENTS. Translated and adapted from the German by C. KEGAN PAUL, M.A., and the Rev. E. D. STONE, M.A. Third Edition. Crown 8vo. 6s.

BELLARS (*Rev. W.*)—THE TESTIMONY OF CONSCIENCE TO THE TRUTH AND DIVINE ORIGIN OF THE CHRISTIAN REVELATION. Burney Prize Essay. Small crown 8vo. 3s. 6d.

BELLASIS (*Edward*)—THE MONEY JAR OF PLAUTUS AT THE ORATORY SCHOOL : An Account of the Recent Representation. With Appendix and 16 Illustrations. Small 4to. 2s.

BELLINGHAM (*Henry*) *M.P.*—SOCIAL ASPECTS OF CATHOLICISM AND PROTESTANTISM IN THEIR CIVIL BEARING UPON NATIONS. Translated and adapted from the French of M. le Baron de Haulleville. With a Preface by his Eminence Cardinal Manning. Second and Cheaper Edition. Crown 8vo. 3s. 6d.

BELLINGHAM (*H. Belsches Graham*)—UPS AND DOWNS OF SPANISH TRAVEL. Second Edition. Crown 8vo. 5s.

BENN (*Alfred W.*)—THE GREEK PHILOSOPHERS. 2 vols. Demy 8vo. 28s.

BENT (*J. Theodore*)—GENOA : How the Republic Rose and Fell. With 18 Illustrations. Demy 8vo. 18s.

BIBLE FOLK-LORE.—A Study in Comparative Mythology. Large crown 8vo. 10s. 6d.

BIRD (Charles) F.G.S.—Higher Education in Germany and England: Being a Brief Practical Account of the Organisation and Curriculum of the German Higher Schools. With Critical Remarks and Suggestions with reference to those of England. Small crown 8vo. 2s. 6d.

BLACKLEY (Rev. W. S.)—Essays on Pauperism. 16mo. cloth, 1s. 6d.; sewed, 1s.

BLECKLY (Henry)—Socrates and the Athenians: an Apology. Crown 8vo. 2s. 6d.

BLOOMFIELD (The Lady)—Reminiscences of Court and Diplomatic Life. New and Cheaper Edition. With Frontispiece. Crown 8vo. 6s.

BLUNT (The Ven. Archdeacon)—The Divine Patriot, and other Sermons, Preached in Scarborough and in Cannes. New and Cheaper Edition. Crown 8vo. 4s. 6d.

BLUNT (Wilfrid S.)—The Future of Islam. Crown 8vo. 6s.

BODDY (Alexander A.)—To Kairwân the Holy. Scenes in Muhammedan Africa. With Route Map, and 8 Illustrations by A. F. Jacassey. Crown 8vo. 6s.

BOOLE (Mary)—Symbolical Methods of Study. Crown 8vo. 5s.

BOUVERIE-PUSEY (S. E. B.)—Permanence and Evolution. An Inquiry into the supposed Mutability of Animal Types. Crown 8vo. 5s.

BOWEN (H. C.) M.A.—Studies in English, for the use of Modern Schools. 7th Thousand. Small crown 8vo. 1s. 6d.

    English Grammar for Beginners. Fcp. 8vo. 1s.

    Simple English Poems. English Literature for Junior Classes. In Four Parts. Parts I., II., and III. 6d. each; Part IV. 1s.; complete, 3s.

BRADLEY (F. H.)—The Principles of Logic. Demy 8vo. 16s.

BRIDGETT (Rev. T. E.)—History of the Holy Eucharist in Great Britain. 2 vols. Demy 8vo. 18s.

BRODRICK (The Hon. G. C.)—Political Studies. Demy 8vo. 14s.

BROOKE (Rev. S. A.)—Life and Letters of the Late Rev. F. W. Robertson, M.A. Edited by:
    I. Uniform with Robertson's Sermons. 2 vols. With Steel Portrait, 7s. 6d.
    II. Library Edition. 8vo. With Portrait, 12s.
    III. A Popular Edition. In 1 vol. 8vo. 6s.

    The Fight of Faith. Sermons preached on various occasions. Fifth Edition. Crown 8vo. 7s. 6d.

    The Spirit of the Christian Life. Third Edition. Crown 8vo. 5s.

    Theology in the English Poets.—Cowper, Coleridge, Wordsworth, and Burns. Fifth Edition. Post 8vo. 5s.

    Christ in Modern Life. Sixteenth Edition. Crown 8vo. 5s.

    Sermons. First Series. Thirteenth Edition. Crown 8vo. 5s.

    Sermons. Second Series. Sixth Edition. Crown 8vo. 5s.

BROWN (Rev. J. Baldwin) B.A.—THE HIGHER LIFE: its Reality, Experience, and Destiny. Sixth Edition. Crown 8vo. 5s.
DOCTRINE OF ANNIHILATION IN THE LIGHT OF THE GOSPEL OF LOVE. Five Discourses. Fourth Edition. Crown 8vo. 2s. 6d.
THE CHRISTIAN POLICY OF LIFE. A Book for Young Men of Business. Third Edition. Crown 8vo. 3s. 6d.
BROWN (S. Borton) B.A.—THE FIRE BAPTISM OF ALL FLESH; or, the Coming Spiritual Crisis of the Dispensation. Crown 8vo. 6s.
BROWN (Horatio F.)—LIFE ON THE LAGOONS. With two Illustrations and a Map. Crown 8vo. 6s.
BROWNBILL (John)—PRINCIPLES OF ENGLISH CANON LAW. Part I. General Introduction. Crown 8vo. 6s.
BROWNE (W. R.)—THE INSPIRATION OF THE NEW TESTAMENT. With a Preface by the Rev. J. P. NORRIS, D.D. Fcp. 8vo. 2s. 6d.
BURDETT (Henry C.)—HELP IN SICKNESS: Where to Go and What to Do. Crown 8vo. 1s. 6d.
HELPS TO HEALTH: The Habitation, The Nursery, The Schoolroom, and The Person. With a Chapter on Pleasure and Health Resorts. Crown 8vo. 1s. 6d.
BURTON (Mrs. Richard)—THE INNER LIFE OF SYRIA, PALESTINE, AND THE HOLY LAND. Post 8vo. 6s.
BUSBECQ (Ogier Ghiselin de)—HIS LIFE AND LETTERS. By CHARLES THORNTON FORSTER, M.A., and F. H. BLACKBURNE DANIELL, M.A. 2 vols. With Frontispieces. Demy 8vo. 24s.
CARPENTER (W. B.) LL.D., M.D., F.R.S., &c.—THE PRINCIPLES OF MENTAL PHYSIOLOGY. With their Applications to the Training and Discipline of the Mind, and the Study of its Morbid Conditions. Illustrated. Sixth Edition. 8vo. 12s.
CATHOLIC DICTIONARY—Containing some account of the Doctrine, Discipline, Rites, Ceremonies, Councils, and Religious Orders of the Catholic Church. By WILLIAM E. ADDIS and THOMAS ARNOLD, M.A. Second Edition, demy 8vo. 21s.
CERVANTES—JOURNEY TO PARNASSUS. Spanish Text, with Translation into English Tercets, Preface, and Illustrative Notes, by JAMES Y. GIBSON. Crown 8vo. 12s.
CHEYNE (Rev. T. K.)—THE PROPHECIES OF ISAIAH. Translated with Critical Notes and Dissertations. 2 vols. Third Edition. Demy 8vo. 25s.
CHICHELE (Mary)—DOING AND UNDOING. A Story. 1 vol. Crown 8vo.
CLAIRAUT—ELEMENTS OF GEOMETRY. Translated by Dr. KAINES. With 145 Figures. Crown 8vo. 4s. 6d.
CLARKE (Rev. Henry James) A.K.C.—THE FUNDAMENTAL SCIENCE. Demy 8vo. 10s. 6d.
CLAYDEN (P. W.)—SAMUEL SHARPE—EGYPTOLOGIST AND TRANSLATOR OF THE BIBLE. Crown 8vo. 6s.
CLIFFORD (Samuel)—WHAT THINK YE OF THE CHRIST? Crown 8vo. 6s.
CLODD (Edward) F.R.A.S.—THE CHILDHOOD OF THE WORLD: a Simple Account of Man in Early Times. Seventh Edition. Crown 8vo. 3s.
A Special Edition for Schools, 1s.

CLODD (Edward)—continued.
  THE CHILDHOOD OF RELIGIONS. Including a Simple Account of the Birth and Growth of Myths and Legends. Eighth Thousand. Crown 8vo. 5s.
  A Special Edition for Schools. 1s. 6d.
  JESUS OF NAZARETH. With a brief sketch of Jewish History to the Time of His Birth. Small crown 8vo. 6s.

COGHLAN (J. Cole) D.D.—THE MODERN PHARISEE, AND OTHER SERMONS. Edited by the Very Rev. H. H. DICKINSON, D.D., Dean of Chapel Royal, Dublin. New and Cheaper Edition. Crown 8vo. 7s. 6d.

COLE (George R. Fitz-Roy)—THE PERUVIANS AT HOME. Crown 8vo. 6s.

COLERIDGE (Sara)—MEMOIR AND LETTERS OF SARA COLERIDGE. Edited by her Daughter. With Index. Cheap Edition. With one Portrait. 7s. 6d.

COLLECTS EXEMPLIFIED (The) — Being Illustrations from the Old and New Testaments of the Collects for the Sundays after Trinity. By the Author of 'A Commentary on the Epistles and Gospels.' Edited by the Rev. JOSEPH JACKSON. Crown 8vo. 5s.

CONNELL (A. K.)—DISCONTENT AND DANGER IN INDIA. Small crown 8vo. 3s. 6d.
  THE ECONOMIC REVOLUTION OF INDIA. Crown 8vo. 4s. 6d.

CORY (William)—A GUIDE TO MODERN ENGLISH HISTORY. Part I.—MDCCCXV.-MDCCCXXX. Demy 8vo. 9s. Part II.—MDCCCXXX.-MDCCCXXXV. 15s.

COTTERILL (H. B.)—AN INTRODUCTION TO THE STUDY OF POETRY. Crown 8vo. 7s. 6d.

COUTTS (Francis Burdett Money)—THE TRAINING OF THE INSTINCT OF LOVE. With a Preface by the Rev. EDWARD THRING, M.A. Small crown 8vo. 2s. 6d.

COX (Rev. Sir George W.) M.A., Bart.—THE MYTHOLOGY OF THE ARYAN NATIONS. New Edition. Demy 8vo. 16s.
  TALES OF ANCIENT GREECE. New Edition. Small crown 8vo. 6s.
  A MANUAL OF MYTHOLOGY IN THE FORM OF QUESTION AND ANSWER. New Edition. Fcp. 8vo. 3s.
  AN INTRODUCTION TO THE SCIENCE OF COMPARATIVE MYTHOLOGY AND FOLK-LORE. Second Edition. Crown 8vo. 7s. 6d.

COX (Rev. Sir G. W.) M.A., Bart., and JONES (Eustace Hinton)—POPULAR ROMANCES OF THE MIDDLE AGES. Third Edition, in 1 vol. Crown 8vo. 6s.

COX (Rev. Samuel) D.D.—A COMMENTARY ON THE BOOK OF JOB. With a Translation. Demy 8vo. 15s.
  SALVATOR MUNDI; or, Is Christ the Saviour of all Men? Ninth Edition. Crown 8vo. 5s.
  THE LARGER HOPE: a Sequel to 'SALVATOR MUNDI.' Second Edition. 16mo. 1s.
  THE GENESIS OF EVIL, AND OTHER SERMONS, mainly expository. Third Edition. Crown 8vo. 6s.

Kegan Paul, Trench, & Co.'s Publications. 7

COX (Rev. Samuel)—continued.
BALAAM : An Exposition and a Study. Crown 8vo. 5s.
MIRACLES. An Argument and a Challenge. Crown 8vo. 2s. 6d.
CRAVEN (Mrs.)—A YEAR'S MEDITATIONS. Crown 8vo. 6s.
CRAWFURD (Oswald)—PORTUGAL, OLD AND NEW. With Illustrations and Maps. New and Cheaper Edition. Crown 8vo. 6s.
CRIME OF CHRISTMAS DAY : A Tale of the Latin Quarter. By the Author of 'My Ducats and My Daughter.' 1s.
CROZIER (John Beattie) M.B.—THE RELIGION OF THE FUTURE. Crown 8vo. 6s.
DANIELL (Clarmont)—THE GOLD TREASURE OF INDIA : An Inquiry into its Amount, the Cause of its Accumulation, and the Proper Means of Using it as Money. Crown 8vo. 5s.
DANISH PARSONAGE. By an Angler. Crown 8vo. 6s.
DARKNESS AND DAWN. The Peaceful Birth of a New Age. Small crown 8vo. 2s. 6d.
DAVIDSON (Rev. Samuel) D.D., LL.D.—CANON OF THE BIBLE : Its Formation, History, and Fluctuations. Third and revised Edition. Small crown 8vo. 5s.
THE DOCTRINE OF LAST THINGS, contained in the New Testament, compared with the Notions of the Jews and the Statements of Church Creeds. Small crown 8vo. 3s. 6d.
DAVIDSON (Thomas)—THE PARTHENON FRIEZE, and other Essays. Crown 8vo. 6s.
DAWSON (Geo.) M.A.—PRAYERS, WITH A DISCOURSE ON PRAYER. Edited by his Wife. First Series. Eighth Edition. Crown 8vo. 6s.
*** Also a New and Cheaper Edition. Crown 8vo. 3s. 6d.
PRAYERS, WITH A DISCOURSE ON PRAYER. Edited by GEORGE ST. CLAIR. Second Series. Crown 8vo. 6s.
SERMONS ON DISPUTED POINTS AND SPECIAL OCCASIONS. Edited by his Wife. Fourth Edition. Crown 8vo. 6s.
SERMONS ON DAILY LIFE AND DUTY. Edited by his Wife. Fourth Edition. Crown 8vo. 6s.
THE AUTHENTIC GOSPEL, and other Sermons. Edited by GEORGE ST. CLAIR. Third Edition. Crown 8vo. 6s.
THREE BOOKS OF GOD. Nature, History, and Scripture. Sermons, Edited by GEORGE ST. CLAIR. Crown 8vo. 6s.
DE JONCOURT (Madame Marie)—WHOLESOME COOKERY. Third Edition. Crown 8vo. 3s. 6d.
DE LONG (Lieut.-Com. G. W.)—THE VOYAGE OF THE 'JEANNETTE.' The Ship and Ice Journals of. Edited by his Wife, EMMA DE LONG. With Portraits, Maps, and many Illustrations on wood and stone. 2 vols. Demy 8vo. 36s.
DEMOCRACY IN THE OLD WORLD AND THE NEW. By the Author of 'The Suez Canal, the Eastern Question, and Abyssinia,' &c. Small crown 8vo. 2s. 6d.
DEVEREUX (W. Cope) R.N., F.R.G.S.—FAIR ITALY, THE RIVIERA AND MONTE CARLO. Comprising a Tour through North and South Italy and Sicily, with a short account of Malta. Crown 8vo. 6s.
DOING AND UNDOING. A Story. By MARY CHICHELE. 1 vol. Crown 8vo.

DOWDEN (Edward) LL.D.—SHAKSPERE : a Critical Study of his Mind and Art. Seventh Edition. Post 8vo. 12s.
STUDIES IN LITERATURE, 1789-1877. Third Edition. Large post 8vo. 6s.

DUFFIELD (A. J.)—DON QUIXOTE : HIS CRITICS AND COMMENTATORS With a brief account of the minor works of MIGUEL DE CERVANTES SAAVEDRA, and a statement of the aim and end of the greatest of them all. A handy book for general readers. Crown 8vo. 3s. 6d.

DU MONCEL (Count)—THE TELEPHONE, THE MICROPHONE, AND THE PHONOGRAPH. With 74 Illustrations. Second Edition. Small crown 8vo. 5s.

DURUY (Victor)—HISTORY OF ROME AND THE ROMAN PEOPLE. Edited by Professor MAHAFFY, with nearly 3,000 Illustrations. 4to. Vols. I., II., and III. in 6 Parts, 30s. each volume.

EDGEWORTH (F. Y.)—MATHEMATICAL PSYCHICS. An Essay on the Application of Mathematics to Social Science. Demy 8vo. 7s. 6d.

EDUCATIONAL CODE OF THE PRUSSIAN NATION, IN ITS PRESENT FORM. In accordance with the Decisions of the Common Provincial Law, and with those of Recent Legislation. Crown 8vo. 2s. 6d.

EDUCATION LIBRARY. Edited by PHILIP MAGNUS :—
AN INTRODUCTION TO THE HISTORY OF EDUCATIONAL THEORIES. By OSCAR BROWNING, M.A. Second Edition. 3s. 6d.
OLD GREEK EDUCATION. By the Rev. Prof. MAHAFFY, M.A. Second Edition. 3s. 6d.
SCHOOL MANAGEMENT ; including a General View of the Work of Education, Organization, and Discipline. By JOSEPH LANDON. Third Edition. Crown 8vo. 6s.

ELSDALE (Henry)—STUDIES IN TENNYSON'S IDYLLS. Crown 8vo. 5s.

ELYOT (Sir Thomas)—THE BOKE NAMED THE GOUERNOUR. Edited from the First Edition of 1531 by HENRY HERBERT STEPHEN CROFT, M.A., Barrister-at-Law. 2 vols. Fcp. 4to. 50s.

EMERSON'S (Ralph Waldo) LIFE. By OLIVER WENDELL HOLMES. [English Copyright Edition.] With Portrait. Crown 8vo. 6s.

ENOCH, THE PROPHET. The Book of. Archbishop Laurence's Translation. With an Introduction by the Author of the 'Evolution of Christianity.' Crown 8vo. 5s.

ERANUS. A COLLECTION OF EXERCISES IN THE ALCAIC AND SAPPHIC METRES. Edited by F. W. CORNISH, Assistant Master at Eton. Second Edition. Crown 8vo. 2s.

EVANS (Mark)—THE STORY OF OUR FATHER'S LOVE, told to Children. Sixth and Cheaper Edition. With Four Illustrations. Fcp. 8vo. 1s. 6d.

'FAN KWAE' AT CANTON BEFORE TREATY DAYS, 1825-1844. By AN OLD RESIDENT. With Frontispiece. Crown 8vo. 5s.

FEIS (Jacob)—SHAKSPERE AND MONTAIGNE : An Endeavour to Explain the Tendency of Hamlet from Allusions in Contemporary Works. Crown 8vo. 5s.

FLECKER (Rev. Eliezer)—SCRIPTURE ONOMATOLOGY. Being Critical Notes on the Septuagint and other versions. Second Edition. Crown 8vo. 3s. 6d.

FLOREDICE (*W. H.*)—A MONTH AMONG THE MERE IRISH. Small crown 8vo. 5s.
FOWLE (*Rev. T. W.*)—THE DIVINE LEGATION OF CHRIST. Crown 8vo. 7s.
FRANK LEWARD. Edited by CHARLES BAMPTON. Crown 8vo. 7s. 6d.
FULLER (*Rev. Morris*)—THE LORD'S DAY; or, Christian Sunday. Its Unity, History, Philosophy, and Perpetual Obligation. Sermons. Demy 8vo. 10s. 6d.
GARDINER (*Samuel R.*) *and J. BASS MULLINGER, M.A.*—INTRODUCTION TO THE STUDY OF ENGLISH HISTORY. Second Edition. Large crown 8vo. 9s.
GARDNER (*Dorsey*) — QUATRE BRAS, LIGNY, AND WATERLOO. A Narrative of the Campaign in Belgium, 1815. With Maps and Plans. Demy 8vo. 16s.
GENESIS IN ADVANCE OF PRESENT SCIENCE. A Critical Investigation of Chapters I. to IX. By a Septuagenarian Beneficed Presbyter. Demy 8vo. 10s. 6d.
GENNA (*E.*)—IRRESPONSIBLE PHILANTHROPISTS. Being some Chapters on the Employment of Gentlewomen. Small crown 8vo. 2s. 6d.
GEORGE (*Henry*)—PROGRESS AND POVERTY: an Inquiry into the Causes of Industrial Depressions, and of Increase of Want with Increase of Wealth. The Remedy. Fifth Library Edition. Post 8vo. 7s. 6d. Cabinet Edition, crown 8vo. 2s. 6d.
  ⁎ Also a Cheap Edition, limp cloth, 1s. 6d.; paper covers, 1s.
  SOCIAL PROBLEMS. Crown 8vo. 5s.
  ⁎ Also a Cheap Edition, paper covers, 1s.
GIBSON (*James Y.*)—JOURNEY TO PARNASSUS. Composed by MIGUEL DE CERVANTES SAAVEDRA. Spanish Text, with Translation into English Tercets, Preface, and Illustrative Notes by. Crown 8vo. 12s.
GLOSSARY OF TERMS AND PHRASES. Edited by the Rev. H. PERCY SMITH and others. Medium 8vo. 12s.
GLOVER (*F.*) *M.A.*—EXEMPLA LATINA. A First Construing Book, with Short Notes, Lexicon, and an Introduction to the Analysis of Sentences. Second Edition. Fcp. 8vo. 2s.
GOLDSMID (*Sir Francis Henry*) *Bart., Q.C., M.P.*—MEMOIR OF. Second Edition, revised. Crown 8vo. 6s.
GOODENOUGH (*Commodore J. G.*)—MEMOIR OF, with Extracts from his Letters and Journals. Edited by his Widow. With Steel Engraved Portrait. Third Edition. Crown 8vo. 5s.
GOSSE (*Edmund*)—STUDIES IN THE LITERATURE OF NORTHERN EUROPE. New Edition. Large post 8vo. 6s.
  SEVENTEENTH CENTURY STUDIES. A Contribution to the History of English Poetry. Demy 8vo. 10s. 6d.
GOULD (*Rev. S. Baring*) *M.A.*—GERMANY, PRESENT AND PAST. New and Cheaper Edition. Large crown 8vo. 7s. 6d.
GOWAN (*Major Walter E.*) — A. IVANOFF'S RUSSIAN GRAMMAR. (16th Edition). Translated, enlarged, and arranged for use of Students of the Russian Language. Demy 8vo. 6s.

GOWER (Lord Ronald)—MY REMINISCENCES. Cheap Edition, with Portrait, Large crown 8vo. 7s. 6d.

GRAHAM (William) M.A.—THE CREED OF SCIENCE, Religious, Moral, and Social. Second Edition, revised. Crown 8vo. 6s.

GREY (Rowland).—IN SUNNY SWITZERLAND. A Tale of Six Weeks. Small crown 8vo. 5s.

GRIFFITH (Thomas) A.M.—THE GOSPEL OF THE DIVINE LIFE: a Study of the Fourth Evangelist. Demy 8vo. 14s.

GRIMLEY (Rev. H. N.) M.A.—TREMADOC SERMONS, CHIEFLY ON THE SPIRITUAL BODY, THE UNSEEN WORLD, AND THE DIVINE HUMANITY. Fourth Edition. Crown 8vo. 6s.

G. S. B.— A STUDY OF THE PROLOGUE AND EPILOGUE IN ENGLISH LITERATURE, from Shakespeare to Dryden. Crown 8vo. 5s.

GUSTAFSON (Axel)—THE FOUNDATION OF DEATH. A Study of the Drink Question. Third Edition. Crown 8vo. 5s.

HAECKEL (Prof. Ernst)—THE HISTORY OF CREATION. Translation revised by Professor E. RAY LANKESTER, M.A., F.R.S. With Coloured Plates and Genealogical Trees of the various groups of both plants and animals. 2 vols. Third Edition. Post 8vo. 32s.

THE HISTORY OF THE EVOLUTION OF MAN. With numerous Illustrations. 2 vols. Post 8vo. 32s.

A VISIT TO CEYLON. Post 8vo. 7s. 6d.

FREEDOM IN SCIENCE AND TEACHING. With a Prefatory Note by T. H. HUXLEY, F.R.S. Crown 8vo. 5s.

HALF-CROWN SERIES :—

A LOST LOVE. By ANNA C. OGLE (Ashford Owen).

SISTER DORA : a Biography. By MARGARET LONSDALE.

TRUE WORDS FOR BRAVE MEN : a Book for Soldiers and Sailors. By the late CHARLES KINGSLEY.

NOTES OF TRAVEL : being Extracts from the Journals of Count VON MOLTKE.

ENGLISH SONNETS. Collected and Arranged by J. DENNIS.

LONDON LYRICS. By F. LOCKER.

HOME SONGS FOR QUIET HOURS. By the Rev. Canon R. H. BAYNES.

HARRIS (William)—THE HISTORY OF THE RADICAL PARTY IN PARLIAMENT. Demy 8vo. 15s.

HARROP (Robert)—BOLINGBROKE. A Political Study and Criticism. Demy 8vo. 14s.

HART (Rev. J. W. T.)—AUTOBIOGRAPHY OF JUDAS ISCARIOT. A Character-Study. Crown 8vo. 3s. 6d.

HAWEIS (Rev. H. R.) M.A.—CURRENT COIN. Materialism—The Devil — Crime — Drunkenness — Pauperism — Emotion — Recreation — The Sabbath. Fifth Edition. Crown 8vo. 5s.

ARROWS IN THE AIR. Fifth Edition. Crown 8vo. 5s.

SPEECH IN SEASON. Fifth Edition. Crown 8vo. 5s.

THOUGHTS FOR THE TIMES. Thirteenth Edition. Crown 8vo. 5s.

UNSECTARIAN FAMILY PRAYERS. New Edition. Fcp. 8vo. 1s. 6d.

HAWKINS (Edwards Comerford)—SPIRIT AND FORM. Sermons preached in the Parish Church of Leatherhead. Crown 8vo. 6s.

HAWTHORNE (Nathaniel)—WORKS. Complete in 12 vols. Large post 8vo. each vol. 7s. 6d.
- VOL. I. TWICE-TOLD TALES.
- II. MOSSES FROM AN OLD MANSE.
- III. THE HOUSE OF THE SEVEN GABLES, and THE SNOW IMAGE.
- IV. THE WONDER BOOK, TANGLEWOOD TALES, and GRANDFATHER'S CHAIR.
- V. THE SCARLET LETTER, and THE BLITHEDALE ROMANCE.
- VI. THE MARBLE FAUN. (Transformation.)
- VII. & VIII. OUR OLD HOME, and ENGLISH NOTE-BOOKS.
- IX. AMERICAN NOTE-BOOKS.
- X. FRENCH AND ITALIAN NOTE-BOOKS.
- XI. SEPTIMIUS FELTON, THE DOLLIVER ROMANCE, FANSHAWE, and, in an appendix, THE ANCESTRAL FOOTSTEP.
- XII. TALES AND ESSAYS, AND OTHER PAPERS, WITH A BIOGRAPHICAL SKETCH OF HAWTHORNE.

HAYES (A. A.) Jun.—NEW COLORADO AND THE SANTA FÉ TRAIL. With Map and 60 Illustrations. Square 8vo. 9s.

HENNESSY (Sir John Pope)—RALEGH IN IRELAND, WITH HIS LETTERS ON IRISH AFFAIRS AND SOME CONTEMPORARY DOCUMENTS. Large crown 8vo. printed on hand-made paper, parchment, 10s. 6d.

HENRY (Philip)—DIARIES AND LETTERS. Edited by MATTHEW HENRY LEE, M.A. Large crown 8vo. 7s. 6d.

HIDE (Albert)—THE AGE TO COME. Small crown 8vo. 2s. 6d.

HIME (Major H. W. L.) R.A.—WAGNERISM: a Protest. Crown 8vo. 2s. 6d.

HINTON (J.)—THE MYSTERY OF PAIN. New Edition. Fcp. 8vo. 1s.
- LIFE AND LETTERS. With an Introduction by Sir W. W. GULL, Bart., and Portrait engraved on Steel by C. H. JEENS. Fifth Edition. Crown 8vo. 8s. 6d.
- PHILOSOPHY AND RELIGION. Selections from the MSS. of the late JAMES HINTON. Edited by CAROLINE HADDON. Second Edition. Crown 8vo. 5s.
- THE LAW BREAKER AND THE COMING OF THE LAW. Edited by MARGARET HINTON. Crown 8vo. 6s.

HODSON OF HODSON'S HORSE; or, Twelve Years of a Soldier's Life in India. Being Extracts from the Letters of the late Major W. S. R. Hodson. With a vindication from the attack of Mr. Bosworth Smith. Edited by his brother, G. H. HODSON, M.A. Fourth Edition. Large crown 8vo. 5s.

HOLTHAM (E. G.)—EIGHT YEARS IN JAPAN, 1873-1881. Work, Travel, and Recreation. With 3 Maps. Large crown 8vo. 9s.

HOMOLOGY OF ECONOMIC JUSTICE: An Essay by an EAST INDIA MERCHANT. Small crown 8vo. 5s.

HOOPER (Mary)—LITTLE DINNERS: HOW TO SERVE THEM WITH ELEGANCE AND ECONOMY. Eighteenth Edition. Crown 8vo. 2s. 6d.
- COOKERY FOR INVALIDS, PERSONS OF DELICATE DIGESTION, AND CHILDREN. Fourth Edition. Crown 8vo. 2s. 6d.
- EVERY-DAY MEALS. Being Economical and Wholesome Recipes for Breakfast, Luncheon, and Supper. Sixth Edition. Crown 8vo. 2s. 6d.

HOPKINS (Ellice)—WORK AMONGST WORKING MEN. Fifth Edition. Crown 8vo. 3s. 6d.

HOSPITALIER (E.)—THE MODERN APPLICATIONS OF ELECTRICITY. Translated and Enlarged by JULIUS MAIER, Ph.D. 2 vols. Second Edition, revised, with many additions and numerous Illustrations. Demy 8vo. 12s. 6d. each volume.

    VOL. I.—Electric Generators, Electric Light.
    II.—Telephone : Various Applications : Electrical Transmission of Energy.

HOUSEHOLD READINGS ON PROPHECY. By A LAYMAN. Small crown 8vo. 3s. 6d.

HUGHES (Henry)—THE REDEMPTION OF THE WORLD. Crown 8vo. 3s. 6d.

HUNTINGFORD (Rev. E.) D.C.L.—THE APOCALYPSE. With a Commentary and Introductory Essay. Demy 8vo. 9s.

HUTCHINSON (H.)—THOUGHT SYMBOLISM AND GRAMMATIC ILLUSIONS : Being a Treatise on the Nature, Purpose, and Material of Speech. Crown 8vo. 5s.

HUTTON (Rev. Charles F.)—UNCONSCIOUS TESTIMONY ; OR, THE SILENT WITNESS OF THE HEBREW TO THE TRUTH OF THE HISTORICAL SCRIPTURES. Crown 8vo. 2s. 6d.

HYNDMAN (H. M.)—THE HISTORICAL BASIS OF SOCIALISM IN ENGLAND. Large crown 8vo. 8s. 6d.

IM THURN (Everard F.)—AMONG THE INDIANS OF GUIANA. Being Sketches, chiefly Anthropologic, from the Interior of British Guiana. With 53 Illustrations and a Map. Demy 8vo. 18s.

JACCOUD (Prof. S.)—THE CURABILITY AND TREATMENT OF PULMONARY PHTHISIS. Translated and Edited by MONTAGU LUBBOCK, M.D. Demy 8vo. 15s.

JAUNT IN A JUNK : A Ten Days' Cruise in Indian Seas. Large crown 8vo. 7s. 6d.

JENKINS (E.) and RAYMOND (J.)—THE ARCHITECT'S LEGAL HANDBOOK. Third Edition, Revised. Crown 8vo. 6s.

JENNINGS (Mrs. Vaughan)— RAHEL : Her Life and Letters. Large post 8vo. 7s. 6d.

JERVIS (Rev. W. Henley)—THE GALLICAN CHURCH AND THE REVOLUTION. A Sequel to the History of the Church of France, from the Concordat of Bologna to the Revolution. Demy 8vo. 18s.

JOEL (L.)—A CONSUL'S MANUAL AND SHIPOWNER'S AND SHIPMASTER'S PRACTICAL GUIDE IN THEIR TRANSACTIONS ABROAD. With Definitions of Nautical, Mercantile, and Legal Terms ; a Glossary of Mercantile Terms in English, French, German, Italian, and Spanish ; Tables of the Money, Weights, and Measures of the Principal Commercial Nations and their Equivalents in British Standards ; and Forms of Consular and Notarial Acts. Demy 8vo. 12s.

JOHNSTONE (C. F.) M.A.—HISTORICAL ABSTRACTS : being Outlines of the History of some of the less known States of Europe. Crown 8vo. 7s. 6d.

JOLLY (*William*) F.R.S.E.—JOHN DUNCAN, Scotch Weaver and Botanist. With Sketches of his Friends and Notices of his Times. With Portrait. Second Edition. Large crown 8vo. 9s.

JONES (C. A.)—THE FOREIGN FREAKS OF FIVE FRIENDS. With 30 Illustrations. Crown 8vo. 6s.

JOYCE (P. W.) LL.D. &c.—OLD CELTIC ROMANCES. Translated from the Gaelic. Crown 8vo. 7s. 6d.

KAUFMANN (*Rev. M.*) B.A.—SOCIALISM: its Nature, its Dangers, and its Remedies considered. Crown 8vo. 7s. 6d.

UTOPIAS; or, Schemes of Social Improvement, from Sir Thomas More to Karl Marx. Crown 8vo. 5s.

KAY (*David*)—EDUCATION AND EDUCATORS. Crown 8vo. 7s. 6d.

KAY (*Joseph*)—FREE TRADE IN LAND. Edited by his Widow. With Preface by the Right Hon. JOHN BRIGHT, M.P. Seventh Edition. Crown 8vo. 5s.

KEMPIS (*Thomas à*)—OF THE IMITATION OF CHRIST. Parchment Library Edition, parchment or cloth, 6s.; vellum, 7s. 6d. The Red Line Edition, fcp. 8vo. red edges, 2s. 6d. The Cabinet Edition, small 8vo. cloth limp, 1s.; or cloth boards, red edges, 1s. 6d. The Miniature Edition, 32mo. red edges, 1s.

*** All the above Editions may be had in various extra bindings.

KENT (C.)—CORONA CATHOLICA AD PETRI SUCCESSORIS PEDES OBLATA. DE SUMMI PONTIFICIS LEONIS XIII. ASSUMPTIONE EPIGRAMMA. In Quinquaginta Linguis. Fcp. 4to. 15s.

KETTLEWELL (*Rev. S.*) M.A.—THOMAS À KEMPIS AND THE BROTHERS OF COMMON LIFE. 2 vols. With Frontispieces. Demy 8vo. 30s.

*** Also an Abridged Edition in 1 vol. With Portrait. Crown 8vo. 7s. 6d.

KIDD (*Joseph*) M.D.—THE LAWS OF THERAPEUTICS; or, the Science and Art of Medicine. Second Edition. Crown 8vo. 6s.

KINGSFORD (*Anna*) M.D.—THE PERFECT WAY IN DIET. A Treatise advocating a Return to the Natural and Ancient Food of Race. Small crown 8vo. 2s.

KINGSLEY (*Charles*) M.A.—LETTERS AND MEMORIES OF HIS LIFE. Edited by his WIFE. With Two Steel Engraved Portraits and Vignettes. Fifteenth Cabinet Edition, in 2 vols. Crown 8vo. 12s.

*** Also a People's Edition in 1 vol. With Portrait. Crown 8vo. 6s.

ALL SAINTS' DAY, and other Sermons. Edited by the Rev. W. HARRISON. Third Edition. Crown 8vo. 7s. 6d.

TRUE WORDS FOR BRAVE MEN. A Book for Soldiers' and Sailors' Libraries. Eleventh Edition. Crown 8vo. 2s. 6d.

KNOX (*Alexander A.*)—THE NEW PLAYGROUND; or, Wanderings in Algeria. New and Cheaper Edition. Large crown 8vo. 6s.

LANDON (*Joseph*)—SCHOOL MANAGEMENT; including a General View of the Work of Education, Organisation, and Discipline. Third Edition. Crown 8vo. 6s.

LAURIE (S. S.)—THE TRAINING OF TEACHERS, and other Educational Papers. Crown 8vo. 7s. 6d.

LEE (Rev. F. G.) D.C.L.—THE OTHER WORLD; or, Glimpses of the Supernatural. 2 vols. A New Edition. Crown 8vo. 15s.

LETTERS FROM AN UNKNOWN FRIEND. By the Author of 'Charles Lowder.' With a Preface by the Rev. W. H. Cleaver. Fcp. 8vo. 1s.

LETTERS FROM A YOUNG EMIGRANT IN MANITOBA. Second Edition. Small crown 8vo. 3s. 6d.

LEWARD (Frank)—Edited by CHAS. BAMPTON. Crown 8vo. 7s. 6d.

LEWIS (Edward Dillon)—A DRAFT CODE OF CRIMINAL LAW AND PROCEDURE. Demy 8vo. 21s.

LILLIE (Arthur) M.R.A.S.—THE POPULAR LIFE OF BUDDHA. Containing an Answer to the Hibbert Lectures of 1881. With Illustrations. Crown 8vo. 6s.

LLOYD (Walter)—THE HOPE OF THE WORLD: An Essay on Universal Redemption. Crown 8vo. 5s.

LONSDALE (Margaret)—SISTER DORA: a Biography. With Portrait. Cheap Edition. Crown 8vo. 2s. 6d.

LOUNSBURY (Thomas R.)—JAMES FENIMORE COOPER. With Portrait. Crown 8vo. 5s.

LOWDER (Charles)—A BIOGRAPHY. By the Author of 'St. Teresa.' New and Cheaper Edition. Crown 8vo. With Portrait. 3s. 6d.

LÜCKES (Eva C. E.)—LECTURES ON GENERAL NURSING, delivered to the Probationers of the London Hospital Training School for Nurses. Crown 8vo. 2s. 6d.

LYALL (William Rowe) D.D.—PROPÆDEIA PROPHETICA; or, The Use and Design of the Old Testament Examined. New Edition, with Notices by GEORGE C. PEARSON, M.A., Hon. Canon of Canterbury. Demy 8vo.

LYTTON (Edward Bulwer, Lord)—LIFE, LETTERS, AND LITERARY REMAINS. By his Son the EARL OF LYTTON. With Portraits, Illustrations, and Facsimiles. Demy 8vo. cloth. Vols. I. and II. 32s.

MACAULAY (G. C.)—FRANCIS BEAUMONT: A Critical Study. Crown 8vo. 5s.

MACCALLUM (M. W.)—STUDIES IN LOW GERMAN AND HIGH GERMAN LITERATURE. Crown 8vo. 6s.

MACHIAVELLI (Niccolò)—HIS LIFE AND TIMES. By Prof. VILLARI. Translated by LINDA VILLARI. 4 vols. Large post 8vo. 48s.

DISCOURSES ON THE FIRST DECADE OF TITUS LIVIUS. Translated from the Italian by NINIAN HILL THOMSON, M.A. Large crown 8vo. 12s.

THE PRINCE. Translated from the Italian by N. H. T. Small crown 8vo. printed on hand-made paper, bevelled boards, 6s.

MACKENZIE (Alexander)—HOW INDIA IS GOVERNED. Being an Account of England's work in India. Small crown 8vo. 2s.

MACNAUGHT (Rev. John)—CŒNA DOMINI: An Essay on the Lord's Supper, its Primitive Institution, Apostolic Uses, and Subsequent History. Demy 8vo. 14s.

MACWALTER (Rev. G. S.)—LIFE OF ANTONIO ROSMINI SERBATI (Founder of the Institute of Charity). 2 vols. Demy 8vo.
[Vol. I. now ready, 12s.

MAGNUS (Mrs.)—ABOUT THE JEWS SINCE BIBLE TIMES. From the Babylonian Exile till the English Exodus. Small crown 8vo. 6s.

MAIR (R. S.) M.D., F.R.C.S.E.—THE MEDICAL GUIDE FOR ANGLO-INDIANS. Being a Compendium of Advice to Europeans in India, relating to the Preservation and Regulation of Health. With a Supplement on the Management of Children in India. Second Edition. Crown 8vo. 3s. 6d.

MALDEN (Henry Elliot)--VIENNA, 1683. The History and Consequences of the Defeat of the Turks before Vienna, September 12, 1683, by John Sobieski, King of Poland, and Charles Leopold, Duke of Lorraine. Crown 8vo. 4s. 6d.

MANY VOICES.—A Volume of Extracts from the Religious Writers of Christendom, from the First to the Sixteenth Century. With Biographical Sketches. Crown 8vo. cloth extra, red edges, 6s.

MARKHAM (Capt. Albert Hastings) R.N.—THE GREAT FROZEN SEA: a Personal Narrative of the Voyage of the *Alert* during the Arctic Expedition of 1875-6. With Six Full-page Illustrations, Two Maps, and Twenty-seven Woodcuts. Sixth and Cheaper Edition. Crown 8vo. 6s.

MARRIAGE AND MATERNITY; or, Scripture Wives and Mothers. Small crown 8vo. 4s. 6d.

MARTINEAU (Gertrude)—OUTLINE LESSONS ON MORALS. Small crown 8vo. 3s. 6d.

MAUDSLEY (H.) M.D.—BODY AND WILL. Being an Essay Concerning Will, in its Metaphysical, Physiological, and Pathological Aspects. 8vo. 12s.

McGRATH (Terence)—PICTURES FROM IRELAND. New and Cheaper Edition. Crown 8vo. 2s.

MEREDITH (M. A.)—THEOTOKOS, THE EXAMPLE FOR WOMAN. Dedicated, by permission, to Lady AGNES WOOD. Revised by the Venerable Archdeacon DENISON. 32mo. 1s. 6d.

MILLER (Edward)—THE HISTORY AND DOCTRINES OF IRVINGISM; or, the so-called Catholic and Apostolic Church. 2 vols. Large post 8vo. 25s.

THE CHURCH IN RELATION TO THE STATE. Large crown 8vo. 7s. 6d.

MINCHIN (J. G.)—BULGARIA SINCE THE WAR: Notes of a Tour in the Autumn of 1879. Small crown 8vo. 3s. 6d.

MITCHELL (Lucy M.)—A HISTORY OF ANCIENT SCULPTURE. With numerous Illustrations, including six Plates in Phototype. Super royal, 42s.

SELECTIONS FROM ANCIENT SCULPTURE. Being a Portfolio containing Reproductions in Phototype of 36 Masterpieces of Ancient Art, to illustrate Mrs. MITCHELL'S 'History of Ancient Sculpture.' 18s.

MITFORD (Bertram)—THROUGH THE ZULU COUNTRY. Its Battlefields and its People. With five Illustrations. Demy 8vo. 14s.

MOCKLER (E.)—A GRAMMAR OF THE BALOOCHEE LANGUAGE, as it is spoken in Makran (Ancient Gedrosia), in the Persia-Arabic and Roman characters. Fcp. 8vo. 5s.

MOLESWORTH (*W. Nassau*)—HISTORY OF THE CHURCH OF ENGLAND FROM 1660. Large crown 8vo. 7s. 6d.

MORELL (*J. R.*)—EUCLID SIMPLIFIED IN METHOD AND LANGUAGE. Being a Manual of Geometry. Compiled from the most important French Works, approved by the University of Paris and the Minister of Public Instruction. Fcp. 8vo. 2s. 6d.

MORRIS (*George*)—THE DUALITY OF ALL DIVINE TRUTH IN OUR LORD JESUS CHRIST: FOR GOD'S SELF-MANIFESTATION IN THE IMPARTATION OF THE DIVINE NATURE TO MAN. Large Crown 8vo. 7s. 6d.

MORSE (*E. S.*) *Ph.D.*—FIRST BOOK OF ZOOLOGY. With numerous Illustrations. New and Cheaper Edition. Crown 8vo. 2s. 6d.

MULL (*Matthias*)—PARADISE LOST. By JOHN MILTON. Books I.-VI. The Mutilations of the Text Emended, the Punctuation Revised, and all Collectively Presented, with Notes and Preface; also a Short Essay on the Intellectual Value of Milton's Works, &c. Demy 8vo. 6s.

MURPHY (*J. N.*)—THE CHAIR OF PETER; or, the Papacy Considered in its Institution, Development, and Organization, and in the Benefits which for over Eighteen Centuries it has conferred on Mankind. Demy 8vo. 18s.

NELSON (*J. H.*) *M.A.*—A PROSPECTUS OF THE SCIENTIFIC STUDY OF THE HINDÛ LAW. Demy 8vo. 9s.

NEWMAN (*Cardinal*)—CHARACTERISTICS FROM THE WRITINGS OF. Being Selections from his various Works. Arranged with the Author's personal Approval. Sixth Edition. With Portrait. Crown 8vo. 6s.
  *** A Portrait of Cardinal Newman, mounted for framing, can be had, 2s. 6d.

NEWMAN (*Francis William*)—ESSAYS ON DIET. Small crown 8vo. 2s.
  2s.
NEW TRUTH AND THE OLD FAITH: ARE THEY INCOMPATIBLE? By a Scientific Layman. Demy 8vo. 10s. 6d.

NEW WERTHER. By LOKI. Small crown 8vo. 2s. 6d.

NICHOLSON (*Edward Byron*)—THE GOSPEL ACCORDING TO THE HEBREWS. Its Fragments Translated and Annotated with a Critical Analysis of the External and Internal Evidence relating to it. Demy 8vo. 9s. 6d.
A NEW COMMENTARY ON THE GOSPEL ACCORDING TO MATTHEW. Demy 8vo. 12s.

NICOLS (*Arthur*) *F.G.S., F.R.G.S.*—CHAPTERS FROM THE PHYSICAL HISTORY OF THE EARTH: an Introduction to Geology and Palæontology With numerous Illustrations. Crown 8vo. 5s.

NOPS (*Marianne*)—CLASS LESSONS ON EUCLID. Part I. containing the First Two Books of the Elements. Crown 8vo. 2s. 6d.

NUCES: EXERCISES ON THE SYNTAX OF THE PUBLIC SCHOOL LATIN PRIMER. New Edition in Three Parts. Crown 8vo. each 1s.
  *** The Three Parts can also be had bound together in cloth, 3s.

OATES (*Frank*) *F.R.G.S.*—MATABELE LAND AND THE VICTORIA FALLS. A Naturalist's Wanderings in the Interior of South Africa. Edited by C. G. OATES, B.A. With numerous Illustrations and 4 Maps. Demy 8vo. 21s.

OGLE (*W.*) *M.D., F.R.C.P.*—ARISTOTLE ON THE PARTS OF ANIMALS. Translated, with Introduction and Notes. Royal 8vo. 12s. 6d.

O'HAGAN (Lord) K.P.— OCCASIONAL PAPERS AND ADDRESSES. Large crown 8vo. 7s. 6d.

OKEN (Lorenz) Life of.—By ALEXANDER ECKER. With Explanatory Notes, Selections from Oken's Correspondence, and Portrait of the Professor. From the German by ALFRED TULK. Crown 8vo. 6s.

O'MEARA (Kathleen)—FREDERIC OZANAM, Professor of the Sorbonne: his Life and Work. Second Edition. Crown 8vo. 7s. 6d.

HENRI PERREYVE AND HIS COUNSELS TO THE SICK. Small crown 8vo. 5s.

OSBORNE (Rev. W. A.)—THE REVISED VERSION OF THE NEW TESTAMENT. A Critical Commentary, with Notes upon the Text. Crown 8vo. 5s.

OTTLEY (Henry Bickersteth)—THE GREAT DILEMMA: Christ His own Witness or His own Accuser. Six Lectures. Second Edition. Crown 8vo. 3s. 6d.

OUR PUBLIC SCHOOLS—ETON, HARROW, WINCHESTER, RUGBY, WESTMINSTER, MARLBOROUGH, THE CHARTERHOUSE. Crown 8vo. 6s.

OWEN (F. M.)—JOHN KEATS: a Study. Crown 8vo. 6s.

ACROSS THE HILLS. Small crown 8vo. 1s. 6d.

OWEN (Rev. Robert) B.D.—SANCTORALE CATHOLICUM; or, Book of Saints. With Notes, Critical, Exegetical, and Historical. Demy 8vo. 18s.

OXENHAM (Rev. F. Nutcombe)—WHAT IS THE TRUTH AS TO EVERLASTING PUNISHMENT? Part II. Being an Historical Enquiry into the Witness and Weight of certain Anti-Origenist Councils. Crown 8vo. 2s. 6d.

OXONIENSIS—ROMANISM, PROTESTANTISM, ANGLICANISM. Being a Layman's View of some Questions of the Day. Together with Remarks on Dr. Littledale's 'Plain Reasons against Joining the Church of Rome.' Small crown 8vo. 3s. 6d.

PALMER (the late William)—NOTES OF A VISIT TO RUSSIA IN 1840–41. Selected and arranged by JOHN H. CARDINAL NEWMAN. With Portrait. Crown 8vo. 8s. 6d.

EARLY CHRISTIAN SYMBOLISM. A series of Compositions from Fresco-Paintings, Glasses, and Sculptured Sarcophagi. Edited by the Rev. PROVOST NORTHCOTE, D.D., and the Rev. CANON BROWNLOW, M.A. With Coloured Plates, folio, 42s.; or with plain plates, folio, 25s.

PARCHMENT LIBRARY. Choicely printed on hand-made paper, limp parchment antique or cloth, 6s.; vellum, 7s. 6d. each volume.

SELECTIONS FROM THE PROSE WRITINGS OF JONATHAN SWIFT. With a Preface and Notes by STANLEY LANE-POOLE, and Portrait.

ENGLISH SACRED LYRICS.

SIR JOSHUA REYNOLDS' DISCOURSES. Edited by EDMUND GOSSE.

SELECTIONS FROM MILTON'S PROSE WRITINGS. Edited by ERNEST MYERS.

THE BOOK OF PSALMS. Translated by the Rev. T. K. CHEYNE, M.A.

THE VICAR OF WAKEFIELD. With Preface and Notes by AUSTIN DOBSON.

ENGLISH COMIC DRAMATISTS. Edited by OSWALD CRAWFURD.

ENGLISH LYRICS.

B

PARCHMENT LIBRARY—continued.
>THE SONNETS OF JOHN MILTON. Edited by MARK PATTISON. With Portrait after Vertue.
>FRENCH LYRICS. Selected and Annotated by GEORGE SAINTSBURY. With miniature Frontispiece, designed and etched by H. G. Glindoni.
>FABLES by MR. JOHN GAY. With Memoir by AUSTIN DOBSON, and an etched Portrait from an unfinished Oil-sketch by Sir Godfrey Kneller.
>SELECT LETTERS OF PERCY BYSSHE SHELLEY. Edited, with an Introtion, by RICHARD GARNETT.
>THE CHRISTIAN YEAR; Thoughts in Verse for the Sundays and Holy Days throughout the Year. With etched Portrait of the Rev. J. Keble, after the Drawing by G. Richmond, R.A.
>SHAKSPERE'S WORKS. Complete in Twelve Volumes.
>EIGHTEENTH CENTURY ESSAYS. Selected and Edited by AUSTIN DOBSON. With a Miniature Frontispiece by R. Caldecott.
>Q. HORATI FLACCI OPERA. Edited by F. A. CORNISH, Assistant Master at Eton. With a Frontispiece after a design by L. ALMA TADEMA. Etched by LEOPOLD LOWENSTAM.
>EDGAR ALLAN POE'S POEMS. With an Essay on his Poetry by ANDREW LANG, and a Frontispiece by Linley Sambourne.
>SHAKSPERE'S SONNETS. Edited by EDWARD DOWDEN. With a Frontispiece etched by Leopold Lowenstam, after the Death Mask.
>ENGLISH ODES. Selected by EDMUND GOSSE. With Frontispiece on India paper by Hamo Thornycroft, A.R.A.
>OF THE IMITATION OF CHRIST. By THOMAS À KEMPIS. A revised Translation. With Frontispiece on India paper, from a Design by W. B. Richmond.
>POEMS: Selected from PERCY BYSSHE SHELLEY. Dedicated to Lady Shelley. With Preface by RICHARD GARNET and a Miniature Frontispiece.
>*₊* The above Volumes may also be had in a variety of leather bindings.

PARSLOE (Joseph) — OUR RAILWAYS. Sketches, Historical and Descriptive. With Practical Information as to Fares and Rates, &c., and a Chapter on Railway Reform. Crown 8vo. 6s.

PASCAL (Blaise)—THE THOUGHTS OF. Translated from the Text of AUGUSTE MOLINIER by C. KEGAN PAUL. Large crown 8vo. with Frontispiece, printed on hand-made paper, parchment antique, or cloth, 12s.; vellum, 15s.

PAUL (C. Kegan)—BIOGRAPHICAL SKETCHES. Printed on hand-made paper, bound in buckram. Second Edition. Crown 8vo. 7s. 6d.

PAUL (Alexander)—SHORT PARLIAMENTS. A History of the National Demand for Frequent General Elections. Small crown 8vo. 3s. 6d.

PEARSON (Rev. S.)—WEEK-DAY LIVING. A Book for Young Men and Women. Second Edition. Crown 8vo. 5s.

PESCHEL (Dr. Oscar)—THE RACES OF MAN AND THEIR GEOGRAPHICAL DISTRIBUTION. Second Edition, large crown 8vo. 9s.

PETERS (F. H.)—THE NICOMACHEAN ETHICS OF ARISTOTLE. Translated by. Crown 8vo. 6s.

PHIPSON (E.)—THE ANIMAL LORE OF SHAKSPEARE'S TIME. Including Quadrupeds, Birds, Reptiles, Fish, and Insects. Large post 8vo. 9s.

Kegan Paul, Trench, & Co.'s Publications. 19

PIDGEON (D.)—An Engineer's Holiday ; or, Notes of a Round Trip from Long. 0° to 0°. New and Cheaper Edition. Large crown 8vo. 7s. 6d.

Old World Questions and New World Answers. Large crown 8vo. 7s. 6d.

Plain Thoughts for Men. Eight Lectures delivered at the Foresters' Hall, Clerkenwell, during the London Mission, 1884. Crown 8vo. 1s. 6d.; paper covers, 1s.

POE (Edgar Allan)—Works of. With an Introduction and a Memoir by Richard Henry Stoddard. In 6 vols. with Frontispieces and Vignettes. Large crown 8vo. 6s. each vol.

POPE (J. Buckingham)—Railway Rates and Radical Rule. Trade Questions as Election Tests. Crown 8vo. 2s. 6d.

PRICE (Prof. Bonamy)—Chapters on Practical Political Economy. Being the Substance of Lectures delivered before the University of Oxford. New and Cheaper Edition. Large post 8vo. 5s.

Pulpit Commentary (The). Old Testament Series. Edited by the Rev. J. S. Exell and the Rev. Canon H. D. M. Spence.

> Genesis. By Rev. T. Whitelaw, M.A. With Homilies by the Very Rev. J. F. Montgomery, D.D., Rev. Prof. R. A. Redford, M.A., LL.B., Rev. F. Hastings, Rev. W. Roberts, M.A. ; an Introduction to the Study of the Old Testament by the Venerable Archdeacon Farrar, D.D., F.R.S. ; and Introductions to the Pentateuch by the Right Rev. H. Cotterill, D.D., and Rev. T. Whitelaw, M.A. Eighth Edition. One vol. 15s.
>
> Exodus. By the Rev. Canon Rawlinson. With Homilies by Rev. J. Orr, Rev. D. Young, Rev. C. A. Goodhart, Rev. J. Urquhart, and Rev. H. T. Robjohns. Fourth Edition. Two vols. 18s.
>
> Leviticus. By the Rev. Prebendary Meyrick, M.A. With Introductions by Rev. R. Collins, Rev. Professor A. Cave, and Homilies by Rev. Prof. Redford, LL.B., Rev. J. A. Macdonald, Rev. W. Clarkson, Rev. S. R. Aldridge, LL.B., and Rev. McCheyne Edgar. Fourth Edition. 15s.
>
> Numbers. By the Rev R. Winterbotham, LL.B. With Homilies by the Rev. Professor W. Binnie, D.D., Rev. E. S. Prout, M.A., Rev. D. Young, Rev. J. Waite ; and an Introduction by the Rev. Thomas Whitelaw, M.A. Fourth Edition. 15s.
>
> Deuteronomy. By Rev. W. L. Alexander, D.D. With Homilies by Rev. D. Davies, M.A., Rev. C. Clemance, D.D., Rev. J. Orr, B.D., and Rev. R. M. Edgar, M.A. Third Edition. 15s.
>
> Joshua. By Rev. J. J. Lias, M.A. With Homilies by Rev. S. R. Aldridge, LL.B., Rev. R. Glover, Rev. E. De Pressensé, D.D., Rev. J. Waite, B.A., Rev. F. W. Adeney, M.A.; and an Introduction by the Rev. A. Plummer, M.A. Fifth Edition. 12s. 6d.
>
> Judges and Ruth. By the Bishop of Bath and Wells and Rev. J. Morison, D.D. With Homilies by Rev. A. F. Muir, M.A., Rev. F. W. Adeney, M.A., Rev. W. M. Statham, and Rev. Professor J. Thomson, M.A. Fourth Edition. 10s. 6d.
>
> 1 Samuel. By the Very Rev. R. P. Smith, D.D. With Homilies by Rev. Donald Fraser, D.D., Rev. Prof. Chapman, and Rev. B. Dale. Sixth Edition. 15s.

B 2

PULPIT COMMENTARY (THE). Old Testament Series—continued.

    1 KINGS. By the Rev. JOSEPH HAMMOND, LL.B. With Homilies by the Rev. E DE PRESSENSÉ, D.D., Rev. J. WAITE, B.A., Rev. A. ROWLAND, LL.B., Rev. J. A. MACDONALD, and Rev. J. URQUHART. Fourth Edition. 15s.

    1 CHRONICLES. By the Rev. Prof. P. C. BARKER, M.A., LL.B. With Homilies by Rev. Prof. J. R. THOMSON, M.A., Rev. R. TUCK, B.A., Rev. W. CLARKSON, B.A., Rev. F. WHITFIELD, M A., and Rev. RICHARD GLOVER. 15s.

    EZRA, NEHEMIAH, AND ESTHER. By Rev. Canon G. RAWLINSON, M.A. With Homilies by Rev. Prof. J. R. THOMSON, M.A., Rev. Prof. R. A. REDFORD, LL.B., M.A., Rev. W. S. LEWIS, M.A., Rev. J. A. MACDONALD, Rev. A. MACKENNAL, B.A., Rev. W. CLARKSON, B.A., Rev. F. HASTINGS, Rev. W. DINWIDDIE, LL.B., Rev. Prof. ROWLANDS, B.A., Rev. G. WOOD, B.A., Rev. Prof. P. C. BARKER, LL.B., M.A., and Rev. J. S. EXELL, M.A. Sixth Edition. One vol. 12s. 6d.

    JEREMIAH (Vol. I.). By the Rev. T. K. CHEYNE, M.A. With Homilies by the Rev. F. W. ADENEY, M.A., Rev. A. F. MUIR, M.A., Rev. S. CONWAY, B.A., Rev. J. WAITE, B.A., and Rev. D. YOUNG, B.A. Second Edition. 15s.

    JEREMIAH (Vol. II.), AND LAMENTATIONS. By Rev. T. K. CHEYNE, M.A. With Homilies by Rev. Prof. J. R. THOMSON, M.A., Rev. W. F. ADENEY, M.A., Rev. A. F. MUIR, M.A., Rev. S. CONWAY, B.A., Rev. D. YOUNG, B.A. 15s.

PULPIT COMMENTARY (THE). New Testament Series.

    ST. MARK. By the Very Rev. E. BICKERSTETH, D.D., Dean of Lichfield. With Homilies by the Rev. Prof. THOMSON, M.A., Rev. Prof. GIVEN, M.A., Rev. Prof. JOHNSON, M.A., Rev. A. ROWLAND, LL.B., Rev. A. MUIR, M.A., and Rev. R. GREEN. Fourth Edition. 2 Vols. 21s.

    THE ACTS OF THE APOSTLES. By the Bishop of BATH AND WELLS. With Homilies by Rev. Prof. P. C. BARKER, M.A., Rev. Prof. E. JOHNSON, M.A., Rev. Prof. R. A. REDFORD, M.A., Rev. R. TUCK, B.A., Rev. W. CLARKSON, B.A. Second Edition. Two vols. 21s.

    1 CORINTHIANS. By the Ven. Archdeacon FARRAR, D.D. With Homilies by Rev. Ex-Chancellor LIPSCOMB, LL.D., Rev. DAVID THOMAS, D.D., Rev. DONALD FRASER, D.D., Rev. Prof. J. R. THOMSON, M.A., Rev. R. TUCK, B.A., Rev. E. HURNDALL, M.A., Rev. J. WAITE, B.A., Rev. H. BREMNER, B.D. Second Edition. 15s.

PUSEY (Dr.)—SERMONS FOR THE CHURCH'S SEASONS FROM ADVENT TO TRINITY. Selected from the published Sermons of the late EDWARD BOUVERIE PUSEY, D.D. Crown 8vo. 5s.

RADCLIFFE (Frank R. Y.)—THE NEW POLITICUS. Small crown 8vo. 2s. 6d.

RANKE (Leopold von)—UNIVERSAL HISTORY. The Oldest Historical Group of Nations and the Greeks. Edited by G. W. PROTHERO. Demy 8vo. 16s.

REALITIES OF THE FUTURE LIFE. Small crown 8vo. 1s. 6d.

RENDELL (J. M.)—CONCISE HANDBOOK OF THE ISLAND OF MADEIRA. With Plan of Funchal and Map of the Island. Fcp. 8vo. 1s. 6d.

REYNOLDS (Rev. J. W.)—THE SUPERNATURAL IN NATURE. A Verification by Free Use of Science. Third Edition, revised and enlarged. Demy 8vo. 14s.

THE MYSTERY OF MIRACLES. Third and Enlarged Edition. Crown 8vo. 6s.

THE MYSTERY OF THE UNIVERSE: Our Common Faith. Demy 8vo. 14s.

RIBOT (Prof. Th.)—HEREDITY: a Psychological Study on its Phenomena, its Laws, its Causes, and its Consequences. Second Edition. Large crown 8vo. 9s.

RIMMER (William) M.D.—ART ANATOMY: A Portfolio of 81 Plates. Folio, 70s. nett.

ROBERTSON (The late Rev. F. W.) M.A.—LIFE AND LETTERS OF. Edited by the Rev. Stopford Brooke, M.A.
   I. Two vols., uniform with the Sermons. With Steel Portrait. Crown 8vo. 7s. 6d.
   II. Library Edition, in demy 8vo. with Portrait. 12s.
   III. A Popular Edition, in 1 vol. Crown 8vo. 6s.

SERMONS. Four Series. Small crown 8vo. 3s. 6d.

THE HUMAN RACE, and other Sermons. Preached at Cheltenham, Oxford, and Brighton. New and Cheaper Edition. Small crown 8vo. 3s. 6d.

NOTES ON GENESIS. New and Cheaper Edition. Small crown 8vo. 3s. 6d.

EXPOSITORY LECTURES ON ST. PAUL'S EPISTLES TO THE CORINTHIANS. A New Edition. Small crown 8vo. 5s.

LECTURES AND ADDRESSES, with other Literary Remains. A New Edition. Small crown 8vo. 5s.

AN ANALYSIS OF TENNYSON'S 'IN MEMORIAM.' (Dedicated by Permission to the Poet-Laureate.) Fcp. 8vo. 2s.

THE EDUCATION OF THE HUMAN RACE. Translated from the German of Gotthold Ephraim Lessing. Fcp. 8vo. 2s. 6d.

The above Works can also be had bound in half-morocco.

** A Portrait of the late Rev. F. W. Robertson, mounted for framing, can be had, 2s. 6d.

ROMANES (G. J.)—MENTAL EVOLUTION IN ANIMALS. With a Posthumous Essay on Instinct, by CHARLES DARWIN, F.R.S. Demy 8vo. 12s.

ROSMINI SERBATI (A.) Founder of the Institute of Charity—LIFE. By G. STUART MACWALTER. 2 vols. 8vo. [Vol. I. now ready, 12s.

ROSMINI'S ORIGIN OF IDEAS. Translated from the Fifth Italian Edition of the Nuovo Saggio. *Sull' origine delle idee.* 3 vols. Demy 8vo. 16s each.

ROSMINI'S PSYCHOLOGY. 3 vols. Demy 8vo. [Vol. I. now ready, 16s.

ROSMINI'S PHILOSOPHICAL SYSTEM. Translated, with a Sketch of the Author's Life, Bibliography, Introduction, and Notes, by THOMAS DAVIDSON. Demy 8vo. 16s.

RULE (Martin) M.A.—THE LIFE AND TIMES OF ST. ANSELM, ARCHBISHOP OF CANTERBURY AND PRIMATE OF THE BRITAINS. 2 vols. Demy 8vo. 32s.

SAMUEL (Sydney M.)—JEWISH LIFE IN THE EAST. Small crown 8vo. 3s. 6d.

SARTORIUS (Ernestine)—THREE MONTHS IN THE SOUDAN. With 11 Full-page Illustrations. Demy 8vo. 14s.

SAYCE (Rev. Archibald Henry)—INTRODUCTION TO THE SCIENCE OF LANGUAGE. 2 vols. Second Edition. Large post 8vo. 21s.

SCIENTIFIC LAYMAN. The New Truth and the Old Faith : are they Incompatible? Demy 8vo. 10s. 6d.

SCOONES (W. Baptiste)—FOUR CENTURIES OF ENGLISH LETTERS : A Selection of 350 Letters by 150 Writers, from the Period of the Paston Letters to the Present Time. Third Edition. Large crown 8vo. 6s.

SÉE (Prof. Germain)—BACILLARY PHTHISIS OF THE LUNGS. Translated and Edited for English Practitioners, by WILLIAM HENRY WEDDELL, M.R.C.S. Demy 8vo.

SHILLITO (Rev. Joseph)—WOMANHOOD : its Duties, Temptations, and Privileges. A Book for Young Women. Third Edition. Crown 8vo. 3s. 6d.

SHIPLEY (Rev. Orby) M.A.—PRINCIPLES OF THE FAITH IN RELATION TO SIN. Topics for Thought in Times of Retreat. Eleven Addresses delivered during a Retreat of Three Days to Persons living in the World. Demy 8vo. 12s.

SIDNEY (Algernon)—A REVIEW. By GERTRUDE M. IRELAND BLACKBURNE. Crown 8vo. 6s.

SISTER AUGUSTINE, Superior of the Sisters of Charity at the St. Johannis Hospital at Bonn. Authorised Translation by HANS THARAU, from the German 'Memorials of AMALIE VON LASAULX.' Cheap Edition. Large crown 8vo. 4s. 6d.

SKINNER (JAMES). A Memoir. By the Author of 'Charles Lowder.' With a Preface by the Rev. Canon CARTER, and Portrait. Large crown 8vo. 7s. 6d.

*** Also a Cheap Edition, with Portrait. Crown 8vo. 3s. 6d.

SMITH (Edward) M.D., LL.B., F.R.S.—TUBERCULAR CONSUMPTION IN ITS EARLY AND REMEDIABLE STAGES. Second Edition. Crown 8vo. 6s.

SPEDDING (James)—REVIEWS AND DISCUSSIONS, LITERARY, POLITICAL, AND HISTORICAL NOT RELATING TO BACON. Demy 8vo. 12s. 6d.

EVENINGS WITH A REVIEWER ; or, Bacon and Macaulay. With a Prefatory Notice by G. S. VENABLES, Q.C. 2 vols. Demy 8vo. 18s.

STAPFER (Paul)—SHAKSPEARE AND CLASSICAL ANTIQUITY : Greek and Latin Antiquity as presented in Shakspeare's Plays. Translated by EMILY J. CAREY. Large post 8vo. 12s.

STATHAM (F. Reginald)—FREE THOUGHT AND TRUE THOUGHT. A Contribution to an Existing Argument. Crown 8vo. 6s.

STEVENSON (Rev. W. F.)—HYMNS FOR THE CHURCH AND HOME. Selected and Edited by the Rev. W. Fleming Stevenson.

The Hymn Book consists of Three Parts :—I. For Public Worship.— II. For Family and Private Worship.—III. For Children.

SMALL EDITION, cloth limp, 10d. ; cloth boards, 1s.
LARGE TYPE EDITION, cloth limp, 1s. 3d. ; cloth boards, 1s. 6d.

STRAY PAPERS ON EDUCATION AND SCENES FROM SCHOOL LIFE. By B. H. Second Edition. Small crown 8vo. 3s. 6d.

STREATFEILD (*Rev. G. S.*) *M.A.*—LINCOLNSHIRE AND THE DANES. Large crown 8vo. 7*s.* 6*d.*

STRECKER-WISLICENUS—ORGANIC CHEMISTRY. Translated and Edited, with Extensive Additions, by W. R. HODGKINSON, Ph.D., and A. J. GREENAWAY, F.I.C. Demy 8vo. 21*s.*

STUDY OF THE PROLOGUE AND EPILOGUE IN ENGLISH LITERATURE, FROM SHAKESPEARE TO DRYDEN. By G. S. B. Crown 8vo. 5*s.*

SULLY (*James*) *M.A.*—PESSIMISM : a History and a Criticism. Second Edition. Demy 8vo. 14*s.*

SUTHERST (*Thomas*).—DEATH AND DISEASE BEHIND THE COUNTER. Crown 8vo. 1*s.* 6*d.* ; paper covers, 1*s.*

SWEDENBORG (*Eman.*)—DE CULTU ET AMORE DEI, UBI AGITUR DE TELLURIS ORTU, PARADISO ET VIVARIO, TUM DE PRIMOGENITI SEU ADAMI NATIVITATE, INFANTIA, ET AMORE. Crown 8vo. 6*s.*

SYME (*David*)—REPRESENTATIVE GOVERNMENT IN ENGLAND : its Faults and Failures. Second Edition. Large crown 8vo. 6*s.*

TACITUS'S AGRICOLA : A Translation. Small crown 8vo. 2*s.* 6*d.*

TAYLOR (*Rev. Isaac*)—THE ALPHABET. An Account of the Origin and Development of Letters. With numerous Tables and Facsimiles. 2 vols. Demy 8vo. 36*s.*

TAYLOR (*Jeremy*)—THE MARRIAGE RING. With Preface, Notes, and Appendices. Edited by FRANCIS BURDETT MONEY COUTTS. Small crown 8vo. 2*s.* 6*d.*

TAYLOR (*Sedley*)—PROFIT SHARING BETWEEN CAPITAL AND LABOUR. To which is added a Memorandum on the Industrial Partnership at the Whitwood Collieries, by ARCHIBALD and HENRY BRIGGS, with Remarks by SEDLEY TAYLOR. Crown 8vo. 2*s.* 6*d.*

THIRTY THOUSAND THOUGHTS. Edited by the Rev. Canon SPENCE, Rev. J. S. EXELL, and Rev. CHARLES NEIL. 6 vols. Super-royal 8vo.
[Vols. I., II., and III. now ready, 16*s.* each.

THOM (*John Hamilton*)—LAWS OF LIFE AFTER THE MIND OF CHRIST. Second Edition. Crown 8vo. 7*s.* 6*d.*

TIDMAN (*Paul F.*)—GOLD AND SILVER MONEY. Part I.—A Plain Statement. Part II.—Objections Answered. Third Edition. Crown 8vo. 1*s.*

TIPPLE (*Rev. S. A.*)—SUNDAY MORNINGS AT NORWOOD. Prayers and Sermons. Crown 8vo. 6*s.*

TODHUNTER (*Dr. J.*)—A STUDY OF SHELLEY. Crown 8vo. 7*s.*

TRANT (*William*)—TRADE UNIONS ; Their Origin and Objects, Influence and Efficacy. Small crown 8vo. 1*s.* 6*d.* ; paper covers, 1*s.*

TREMENHEERE (*H. Seymour*) *C.B.*—A MANUAL OF THE PRINCIPLES OF GOVERNMENT AS SET FORTH BY THE AUTHORITIES OF ANCIENT AND MODERN TIMES. New and enlarged Edition. Crown 8vo. 3*s.* 6*d.*

TUKE (*Daniel Hack*) *M.D.*—CHAPTERS IN THE HISTORY OF THE INSANE IN THE BRITISH ISLES. With Four Illustrations. Large crown 8vo. 12*s.*

TWINING (*Louisa*)—WORKHOUSE VISITING AND MANAGEMENT DURING TWENTY-FIVE YEARS. Small crown 8vo. 2*s.*

TYLER (J.)—THE MYSTERY OF BEING; OR, WHAT DO WE KNOW? Small crown 8vo. 3s. 6d.

UPTON (Major R. D.)—GLEANINGS FROM THE DESERT OF ARABIA. Large post 8vo. 10s. 6d.

VACUUS VIATOR—FLYING SOUTH. Recollections of France and its Littoral. Small crown 8vo. 3s. 6d.

VAUGHAN (H. Halford)—NEW READINGS AND RENDERINGS OF SHAKESPEARE'S TRAGEDIES. 2 vols. Demy 8vo. 25s.

VILLARI (Professor)—NICCOLÒ MACHIAVELLI AND HIS TIMES. Translated by Linda Villari. 4 vols. Large crown 8vo. 48s.

VILLIERS (The Right Hon. C. P.)—FREE TRADE SPEECHES OF. With Political Memoir. Edited by a Member of the Cobden Club. 2 vols. With Portrait. Demy 8vo. 25s.

** Also a People's Edition, in 1 vol. crown 8vo. limp 2s. 6d.

VOGT (Lieut.-Col. Hermann)—THE EGYPTIAN WAR OF 1882. A Translation. With Map and Plans. Large crown 8vo. 6s.

VOLCKXSOM (E. W. v.)—CATECHISM OF ELEMENTARY MODERN CHEMISTRY. Small crown 8vo. 3s.

VYNER (Lady Mary)—EVERY DAY A PORTION. Adapted from the Bible and the Prayer Book, for the Private Devotions of those living in Widowhood. Collected and Edited by Lady Mary Vyner. Square crown 8vo. 5s.

WALDSTEIN (Charles) Ph.D.—THE BALANCE OF EMOTION AND INTELLECT; an Introductory Essay to the Study of Philosophy. Crown 8vo. 6s.

WALLER (Rev. C. B.)—THE APOCALYPSE, reviewed under the Light of the Doctrine of the Unfolding Ages, and the Restitution of All Things. Demy 8vo. 12s.

WALPOLE (Chas. George)—A SHORT HISTORY OF IRELAND FROM THE EARLIEST TIMES TO THE UNION WITH GREAT BRITAIN. With 5 Maps and Appendices. Second Edition. Crown 8vo. 6s.

WALSHE (Walter Hayle) M.D.—DRAMATIC SINGING PHYSIOLOGICALLY ESTIMATED. Crown 8vo. cloth, price 3s. 6d.

WARD (William George) Ph.D.— ESSAYS ON THE PHILOSOPHY OF THEISM. Edited, with an Introduction, by WILFRID WARD. 2 vols. demy 8vo. 21s.

WARD (Wilfrid)—THE WISH TO BELIEVE: A Discussion concerning the Temper of Mind in which a reasonable Man should undertake Religious Inquiry. Small crown 8vo. 5s.

WEDDERBURN (Sir David) Bart., M.P.—LIFE OF. Compiled from his Journals and Writings by his Sister, Mrs. E. H. PERCIVAL. With etched Portrait, and facsimiles of Pencil Sketches. Demy 8vo. 14s.

WEDMORE (Frederick)—THE MASTERS OF GENRE PAINTING. With Sixteen Illustrations. Post 8vo. 7s. 6d.

WHAT TO DO AND HOW TO DO IT. A Manual of the Law affecting the Housing and Sanitary Condition of Londoners, with Special Reference to the Dwellings of the Poor. Issued by the Sanitary Laws Enforcement Society. Demy 8vo. 1s.

WHEWELL (William) D.D.—HIS LIFE AND SELECTIONS FROM HIS CORRESPONDENCE. By Mrs. STAIR DOUGLAS. With a Portrait from a Painting by SAMUEL LAURENCE. Demy 8vo. 21s.

WHITNEY (Prof. William Dwight)—ESSENTIALS OF ENGLISH GRAMMAR, for the Use of Schools. Second Edition, crown 8vo. 3s. 6d.

WILLIAMS (Rowland) D.D.—PSALMS, LITANIES, COUNSELS, AND COLLECTS FOR DEVOUT PERSONS. Edited by his Widow. New and Popular Edition. Crown 8vo. 3s. 6d.

STRAY THOUGHTS COLLECTED FROM THE WRITINGS OF THE LATE ROWLAND WILLIAMS, D.D. Edited by his Widow. Crown 8vo. 3s. 6d.

WILSON (Lieut.-Col. C. T.)—THE DUKE OF BERWICK, MARSHAL OF FRANCE, 1702-1734. Demy 8vo. 15s.

WILSON (Mrs. R. F.)—THE CHRISTIAN BROTHERS : THEIR ORIGIN AND WORK. With a Sketch of the Life of their Founder, the Ven. Jean Baptiste, de la Salle. Crown 8vo. 6s.

WOLTMANN (Dr. Alfred), and WOERMANN (Dr. Karl)— HISTORY OF PAINTING. Edited by Sidney Colvin. Vol. I. Painting in Antiquity and the Middle Ages. With numerous Illustrations. Medium 8vo. 28s.; bevelled boards, gilt leaves, 30s.

WORD WAS MADE FLESH. Short Family Readings on the Epistles for each Sunday of the Christian Year. Demy 8vo. 10s. 6d.

WREN (Sir Christopher)—HIS FAMILY AND HIS TIMES. With Original Letters, and a Discourse on Architecture hitherto unpublished. By LUCY PHILLIMORE. Demy 8vo. 10s. 6d.

YOUMANS (Eliza A.)—FIRST BOOK OF BOTANY. Designed to cultivate the Observing Powers of Children. With 300 Engravings. New and Cheaper Edition. Crown 8vo. 2s. 6d.

YOUMANS (Edward L.) M.D.—A CLASS BOOK OF CHEMISTRY, on the Basis of the New System. With 200 Illustrations. Crown 8vo. 5s.

THE INTERNATIONAL SCIENTIFIC SERIES.

I. FORMS OF WATER: a Familiar Exposition of the Origin and Phenomena of Glaciers. By J. Tyndall, LL.D., F.R.S. With 25 Illustrations. Eighth Edition. Crown 8vo. 5s.

II. PHYSICS AND POLITICS; or, Thoughts on the Application of the Principles of 'Natural Selection' and 'Inheritance' to Political Society. By Walter Bagehot. Sixth Edition. Crown 8vo. 4s.

III. FOODS. By Edward Smith, M.D., LL.B., F.R.S. With numerous Illustrations. Eighth Edition. Crown 8vo. 5s.

IV. MIND AND BODY: the Theories of their Relation. By Alexander Bain, LL.D. With Four Illustrations. Seventh Edition. Crown 8vo. 4s.

V. THE STUDY OF SOCIOLOGY. By Herbert Spencer. Eleventh Edition. Crown 8vo. 5s.

VI. ON THE CONSERVATION OF ENERGY. By Balfour Stewart, M.A., LL.D., F.R.S. With 14 Illustrations. Sixth Edition. Crown 8vo. 5s.

VII. ANIMAL LOCOMOTION; or, Walking, Swimming, and Flying. By J. B. Pettigrew, M.D., F.R.S., &c. With 130 Illustrations. Third Edition. Crown 8vo. 5s.

VIII. RESPONSIBILITY IN MENTAL DISEASE. By Henry Maudsley, M.D. Fourth Edition. Crown 8vo. 5s.

IX. THE NEW CHEMISTRY. By Professor J. P. Cooke. With 31 Illustrations. Eighth Edition, remodelled and enlarged. Crown 8vo. 5s.

X. THE SCIENCE OF LAW. By Professor Sheldon Amos. Fifth Edition. Crown 8vo. 5s.

XI. ANIMAL MECHANISM: a Treatise on Terrestrial and Aërial Locomotion. By Professor E. J. Marey. With 117 Illustrations. Third Edition. Crown 8vo. 5s.

XII. THE DOCTRINE OF DESCENT AND DARWINISM. By Professor Oscar Schmidt. With 26 Illustrations. Sixth Edition. Crown 8vo. 5s.

XIII. THE HISTORY OF THE CONFLICT BETWEEN RELIGION AND SCIENCE. By J. W. Draper, M.D., LL.D. Eighteenth Edition. Crown 8vo. 5s.

XIV. FUNGI: their Nature, Influences, Uses, &c. By M. C. Cooke, M.D., LL.D. Edited by the Rev. M. J. Berkeley, M.A., F.L.S. With numerous Illustrations. Third Edition. Crown 8vo. 5s.

XV. THE CHEMICAL EFFECTS OF LIGHT AND PHOTOGRAPHY. By Dr. Hermann Vogel. Translation thoroughly revised. With 100 Illustrations. Fourth Edition. Crown 8vo. 5s.

XVI. THE LIFE AND GROWTH OF LANGUAGE. By Professor William Dwight Whitney. Fourth Edition. Crown 8vo. 5s.

XVII. MONEY AND THE MECHANISM OF EXCHANGE. By W. Stanley Jevons, M.A., F.R.S. Sixth Edition. Crown 8vo. 5s.

XVIII. THE NATURE OF LIGHT. With a General Account of Physical Optics. By Dr. Eugene Lommel. With 188 Illustrations and a Table of Spectra in Chromo-lithography. Third Edit. Crown 8vo. 5s.

XIX. ANIMAL PARASITES AND MESSMATES. By P. J. Van Beneden. With 83 Illustrations. Third Edition. Crown 8vo. 5s.

XX. FERMENTATION. By Professor Schützenberger. With 28 Illustrations. Fourth Edition. Crown 8vo. 5s.

XXI. THE FIVE SENSES OF MAN. By Professor Bernstein. With 91 Illustrations. Fourth Edition. Crown 8vo. 5s.

XXII. THE THEORY OF SOUND IN ITS RELATION TO MUSIC. By Professor Pietro Blaserna. With numerous Illustrations. Third Edition. Crown 8vo. 5s.

XXIII. STUDIES IN SPECTRUM ANALYSIS. By J. Norman Lockyer, F.R.S. Third Edition. With six Photographic Illustrations of Spectra, and numerous Engravings on Wood. Crown 8vo. 6s. 6d.

XXIV. A History of the Growth of the Steam Engine. By Professor R. H. Thurston. With numerous Illustrations. Third Edition. Crown 8vo. 6s. 6d.

XXV. Education as a Science. By Alexander Bain, LL.D. Fourth Edition. Crown 8vo. 5s.

XXVI. The Human Species. By Prof. A. De Quatrefages. Third Edition. Crown 8vo. 5s.

XXVII. Modern Chromatics. With Applications to Art and Industry. By Ogden N. Rood. With 130 original Illustrations. Second Edition. Crown 8vo. 5s.

XXVIII. The Crayfish: an Introduction to the Study of Zoology. By Professor T. H. Huxley. With 82 Illustrations. Fourth Edition. Crown 8vo. 5s.

XXIX. The Brain as an Organ of Mind. By H. Charlton Bastian, M.D. With numerous Illustrations. Third Edition. Crown 8vo. 5s.

XXX. The Atomic Theory. By Prof. Wurtz. Translated by G. Cleminshaw, F.C.S. Third Edition. Crown 8vo. 5s.

XXXI. The Natural Conditions of Existence as they affect Animal Life. By Karl Semper. With 2 Maps and 106 Woodcuts. Third Edition. Crown 8vo. 5s.

XXXII. General Physiology of Muscles and Nerves. By Prof. J. Rosenthal. Third Edition. With Illustrations. Crown 8vo. 5s.

XXXIII. Sight: an Exposition of the Principles of Monocular and Binocular Vision. By Joseph Le Conte, LL.D. Second Edition. With 132 Illustrations. Crown 8vo. 5s.

XXXIV. Illusions: a Psychological Study. By James Sully. Second Edition. Crown 8vo. 5s.

XXXV. Volcanoes: what they are and what they teach. By Professor J. W. Judd, F.R.S. With 92 Illustrations on Wood. Third Edition. Crown 8vo. 5s.

XXXVI. Suicide: an Essay on Comparative Moral Statistics. By Prof. H. Morselli. Second Edition. With Diagrams. Crown 8vo. 5s.

XXXVII. The Brain and its Functions. By J. Luys. Second Edition. With Illustrations. Crown 8vo. 5s.

XXXVIII. Myth and Science: an Essay. By Tito Vignoli. Second Edition. Crown 8vo. 5s.

XXXIX. The Sun. By Professor Young. With Illustrations. Second Edition. Crown 8vo. 5s.

XL. Ants, Bees, and Wasps: a Record of Observations on the Habits of the Social Hymenoptera. By Sir John Lubbock, Bart., M.P. With 5 Chromolithographic Illustrations. Seventh Edition. Crown 8vo. 5s.

XLI. Animal Intelligence. By G. J. Romanes, LL.D., F.R.S. Third Edition. Crown 8vo. 5s.

XLII. The Concepts and Theories of Modern Physics. By J. B. Stallo. Third Edition. Crown 8vo. 5s.

XLIII. Diseases of Memory: an Essay in the Positive Pyschology. By Prof. Th. Ribot. Second Edition. Crown 8vo. 5s.

XLIV. Man before Metals. By N. Joly. Third Edition. Crown 8vo. 5s.

XLV. The Science of Politics. By Prof. Sheldon Amos. Third Edit. Crown. 8vo. 5s.

XLVI. Elementary Meteorology. By Robert H. Scott. Third Edition. With numerous Illustrations. Crown 8vo. 5s.

XLVII. The Organs of Speech and their Application in the Formation of Articulate Sounds. By Georg Hermann von Meyer. With 47 Woodcuts. Crown 8vo. 5s.

XLVIII. Fallacies: a View of Logic from the Practical Side. By Alfred Sidgwick. Crown 8vo. 5s.

XLIX. Origin of Cultivated Plants. By Alphonse de Candolle. Crown 8vo. 5s.

L. Jelly Fish, Star Fish, and Sea Urchins. Being a Research on Primitive Nervous Systems. By G. J. Romanes. Crown 8vo. 5s.

MILITARY WORKS.

BARRINGTON (Capt. J. T.)—ENGLAND ON THE DEFENSIVE; or, the Problem of Invasion Critically Examined. Large crown 8vo. with Map, 7s. 6d.

BRACKENBURY (Col. C. B.) R.A.—MILITARY HANDBOOKS FOR REGIMENTAL OFFICERS:

I. MILITARY SKETCHING AND RECONNAISSANCE. By Colonel F. J. Hutchison and Major H. G. MacGregor. Fourth Edition. With 15 Plates. Small crown 8vo. 4s.

II. THE ELEMENTS OF MODERN TACTICS PRACTICALLY APPLIED TO ENGLISH FORMATIONS. By Lieut.-Col. Wilkinson Shaw. Fifth Edit. With 25 Plates and Maps. Small crown 8vo. 9s.

III. FIELD ARTILLERY: its Equipment, Organisation, and Tactics. By Major Sisson C. Pratt, R.A. With 12 Plates. Second Edition. Small crown 8vo. 6s.

IV. THE ELEMENTS OF MILITARY ADMINISTRATION. First Part: Permanent System of Administration. By Major J. W. Buxton. Small crown 8vo. 7s. 6d.

V. MILITARY LAW: its Procedure and Practice. By Major Sisson C. Pratt, R.A. Second Edition. Small crown 8vo. 4s. 6d.

VI. CAVALRY IN MODERN WAR. By Col. F. Chenevix Trench. Small crown 8vo. 6s.

VII. FIELD WORKS. Their Technical Construction and Tactical Application. By the Editor, Col. C. B. Brackenbury, R.A. Small crown 8vo.

BROOKE (Major C. K.)—A SYSTEM OF FIELD TRAINING. Small crown 8vo. 2s.

CLERY (C.) Lieut.-Col.—MINOR TACTICS. With 26 Maps and Plans. Sixth and cheaper Edition, revised. Crown 8vo. 9s.

COLVILE (Lieut.-Col. C. F.)—MILITARY TRIBUNALS. Sewed, 2s. 6d.

CRAUFURD (Capt. H. J.)—SUGGESTIONS FOR THE MILITARY TRAINING OF A COMPANY OF INFANTRY. Crown 8vo. 1s. 6d.

HARRISON (Lieut.-Col. R.) — THE OFFICER'S MEMORANDUM BOOK FOR PEACE AND WAR. Third Edition. Oblong 32mo. roan, with pencil, 3s. 6d.

NOTES ON CAVALRY TACTICS, ORGANISATION, &c. By a Cavalry Officer. With Diagrams. Demy 8vo. 12s.

PARR (Capt. H. Hallam) C.M.G.—THE DRESS, HORSES, AND EQUIPMENT OF INFANTRY AND STAFF OFFICERS. Crown 8vo. 1s.

SCHAW (Col. H.)—THE DEFENCE AND ATTACK OF POSITIONS AND LOCALITIES. Third Edition, revised and corrected. Crown 8vo. 3s. 6d.

WILKINSON (H. Spenser) Capt. 20th Lancashire R.V.—CITIZEN SOLDIERS. Essays towards the Improvement of the Volunteer Force. Crown 8vo. 2s. 6d.

POETRY.

ADAM OF ST. VICTOR—THE LITURGICAL POETRY OF ADAM OF ST. VICTOR. From the text of Gautier. With Translations into English in the Original Metres, and Short Explanatory Notes. By Digby S. Wrangham, M.A. 3 vols. Crown 8vo. printed on hand-made paper, boards, 21s.

AUCHMUTY (A. C.)—POEMS OF ENGLISH HEROISM: From Brunanburgh to Lucknow; from Athelstan to Albert. Small crown 8vo. 1s. 6d.

AVIA—THE ODYSSEY OF HOMER. Done into English Verse by. Fcp. '4to. 15s.

BARING (T. C.), M.P.—THE SCHEME OF EPICURUS. A Rendering into English Verse of the Unfinished Poem of Lucretius, entitled, 'De Rerum Naturâ.' Fcp. 4to. 7s.

BARNES (William)—POEMS OF RURAL LIFE, IN THE DORSET DIALECT. New Edition, complete in one vol. Crown 8vo. 8s. 6d.

BAYNES (Rev. Canon H. R.)—HOME SONGS FOR QUIET HOURS. Fourth and cheaper Edition. Fcp. 8vo. 2s. 6d.

BENDALL (Gerard)—MUSA SILVESTRIS. 16mo. 1s. 6d.

BEVINGTON (L. S.)—KEY NOTES. Small crown 8vo. 5s.

BILLSON (C. J.)—THE ACHARNIANS OF ARISTOPHANES. Crown 8vo. 3s. 6d.

BLUNT (Wilfrid Scawen)—THE WIND AND THE WHIRLWIND. Demy 8vo. 1s. 6d.

BOWEN (H. C.) M.A.—SIMPLE ENGLISH POEMS. English Literature for Junior Classes. In Four Parts. Parts I. II. and III. 6d. each, and Part IV. 1s., complete 3s.

BRASHER (Alfred)—SOPHIA; or, the Viceroy of Valencia. A Comedy in Five Acts, Founded on a Story in Scarron. Small crown 8vo. 2s. 6d.

BRYANT (W. C.) — POEMS. Cheap Edition, with Frontispiece. Small crown 8vo. 3s. 6d.

BYRNNE (E. Fairfax)—MILICENT: a Poem. Small crown 8vo. 6s.

CAILLARD (Emma Marie) — CHARLOTTE CORDAY, and other Poems. Small crown 8vo. 3s. 6d.

CALDERON'S DRAMAS: the Wonder-working Magician—Life is a Dream—the Purgatory of St. Patrick. Translated by Denis Florence MacCarthy. Post 8vo. 10s.

CAMOENS LUSIADS. Portuguese Text with English Translation, by J. J. AUBERTIN. Second Edition. 2 vols. Crown 8vo. 12s.

CAMPBELL (Lewis)—SOPHOCLES. The Seven Plays in English Verse. Crown 8vo. 7s. 6d.

CASTILIAN BROTHERS (The) —CHATEAUBRIANT, WALDEMAR, THREE TRAGEDIES, AND THE ROSE OF SICILY. A Drama. By the Author of 'Ginevra,' &c. Crown 8vo. 6s.

CHRISTIAN (Owen)—POEMS. Small crown 8vo. 2s. 6d.

CHRONICLES OF CHRISTOPHER COLUMBUS; a Poem in Twelve Cantos. By M. D. C. Crown 8vo. 7s. 6d.

CLARKE (Mary Cowden)—HONEY FROM THE WEED. Verses. Crown 8vo. 7s.

COSMO DE MEDICI, The False One, Agramont and Beaumont, Three Tragedies, and The Deformed. A Dramatic Sketch. By the Author of 'Ginevra,' &c. Crown 8vo. 5s.

COXHEAD (Ethel)—BIRDS AND BABIES. Imp. 16mo. With 33 Illustrations. 2s. 6d.

DAVID RIZZIO, BOTHWELL, AND THE WITCH LADY. Three Tragedies. By the Author of 'Ginevra,' &c. Crown 8vo. 6s.

DAVIE (G. S.) M.D.—THE GARDEN OF FRAGRANCE. Being a complete Translation of the Bóstan of Sádi, from the original Persian into English Verse. Crown 8vo. 7s. 6d.

DAVIES (T. Hart)—CATULLUS. Translated into English Verse. Crown 8vo. 6s.

DENNIS (J.) — ENGLISH SONNETS. Collected and Arranged by. Small crown 8vo. 2s. 6d.

DE VERE (Aubrey)—POETICAL WORKS:

    I. THE SEARCH AFTER PROSERPINE, &c. 6s.

    II. THE LEGENDS OF ST. PATRICK, &c. 6s.

    III. ALEXANDER THE GREAT, &c. 6s.

DE VERE (Aubrey)—continued.
THE FORAY OF QUEEN MEAVE, and other Legends of Ireland's Heroic Age. Small crown 8vo. 5s.
LEGENDS OF THE SAXON SAINTS. Small crown 8vo. 6s.

DILLON (Arthur)—RIVER SONGS and other Poems. With 13 Autotype Illustrations from designs by Margery May. Fcp. 4to. cloth extra, gilt leaves, 10s. 6d.

DOBELL (Mrs. Horace)—ETHELSTONE, EVELINE, and other Poems. Crown 8vo. 6s.

DOBSON (Austin)—OLD WORLD IDYLLS, and other Verses. Fourth Edition. 18mo. cloth extra, gilt tops, 6s.

DOMET (Alfred)—RANOLF AND AMOHIA: a Dream of Two Lives. New Edition revised. 2 vols. Crown 8vo. 12s.

DOROTHY: a Country Story in Elegiac Verse. With Preface. Demy 8vo. 5s.

DOWDEN (Edward) LL.D.—SHAKSPERE'S SONNETS. With Introduction and Notes. Large post 8vo. 7s. 6d.

DUTT (Toru)—A SHEAF GLEANED IN FRENCH FIELDS. New Edition. Demy 8vo. 10s. 6d.

EDMONDS (E. M.) — HESPERAS. Rhythm and Rhyme. Crown 8vo. 4s.

EDWARDS (Miss Betham) — POEMS. Small crown 8vo. 3s. 6d.

ELDRYTH (Maud)—MARGARET, and other Poems. Small crown 8vo. 3s. 6d.
ALL SOULS' EVE, 'NO GOD,' and other Poems. Fcp. 8vo. 3s. 6d.

ELLIOTT (Ebenezer), The Corn Law Rhymer—POEMS. Edited by his Son, the Rev. Edwin Elliott, of St. John's, Antigua. 2 vols. crown 8vo. 8s.

ENGLISH VERSE. Edited by W. J. LINTON and R. H. STODDARD. In 5 vols. Crown 8vo. each 5s.
 1. CHAUCER TO BURNS.
 2. TRANSLATIONS.
 3. LYRICS OF THE NINETEENTH CENTURY.
 4. DRAMATIC SCENES AND CHARACTERS.
 5. BALLADS AND ROMANCES.

ENIS—GATHERED LEAVES. Small crown 8vo.

EVANS (Anne)—POEMS AND MUSIC. With Memorial Preface by ANN THACKERAY RITCHIE. Large crown 8vo. 7s.

FORSTER (the late William)—MIDAS. Crown 8vo. 5s.

GINNER (Isaac B.)—THE DEATH OF OTHO, and other Poems. Small crown 8vo. 5s.

GOODCHILD (John A.) — SOMNIA MEDICI. Small crown 8vo. 5s.

GOSSE (Edmund W.)—NEW POEMS. Crown 8vo. 7s. 6d.

GRAHAM (William) — TWO FANCIES, and other Poems. Crown 8vo. 5s.

GRINDROD (Charles) — PLAYS FROM ENGLISH HISTORY. Crown 8vo. 7s. 6d.

THE STRANGER'S STORY and his Poem, THE LAMENT OF LOVE: An Episode of the Malvern Hills. Small crown 8vo. 2s. 6d.

GURNEY (Rev. Alfred)—THE VISION OF THE EUCHARIST, and other Poems. Crown 8vo. 5s.

A CHRISTMAS FAGGOT. Small crown 8vo. 5s.

HELLON (H. G.) - DAPHNIS: a Pastoral Poem. Small crown 8vo. 3s. 6d.

HENRY (Daniel) junr. — UNDER A FOOL'S CAP. Songs. Crown 8vo. bevelled boards, 5s.

HERMAN WALDGRAVE: a Life's Drama. By the Author of 'Ginevra,' &c. Crown 8vo. 6s.

HEYWOOD (J. C.) — HERODIAS. A Dramatic Poem. New Edition revised. Small crown 8vo. 5s.

HICKEY (E. H.)—A SCULPTOR, and other Poems. Small crown 8vo. 5s.

HONEYWOOD (Patty)—POEMS. Dedicated, by permission, to Lord Wolseley, G.C.B., &c. Small crown 8vo. 2s. 6d.

JENKINS (Rev. Canon) — ALFONSO PETRUCCI, Cardinal and Conspirator : an Historical Tragedy in Five Acts. Small crown 8vo. 3*s.* 6*d.*

JOHNSON (Ernle S. W.)—ILARIA, and other Poems. Small crown 8vo. 3*s.*6*d.*

KEATS (John) — POETICAL WORKS. Edited by W. T. ARNOLD. Large crown 8vo. choicely printed on hand-made paper, with Portrait in *eau forte*. Parchment, or cloth, 12*s.* ; vellum, 15*s.*

KENNEDY (Capt. Alexander W. M. Clark) — ROBERT THE BRUCE. A Poem : Historical and Romantic. With 3 Illustrations by James Faed, Junr. Printed on hand-made paper, parchment, bevelled boards, crown 8vo. 10*s.* 6*d.*

KING (Edward)—ECHOES FROM THE ORIENT. With Miscellaneous Poems. Small crown 8vo. 3*s.* 6*d.*

KING (Mrs. Hamilton)—THE DISCIPLES. Sixth Edition, with Portrait and Notes. Crown 8vo. 5*s.*

A BOOK OF DREAMS. Crown 8vo. 3*s.*6*d.*

KNOX (The Hon. Mrs. O. N.)—FOUR PICTURES FROM A LIFE, and other Poems. Small crown 8vo. 3*s.* 6*d.*

LANG (A.)—XXXII BALLADES IN BLUE CHINA. Elzevir 8vo. parchment, or cloth, 5*s.*

RHYMES À LA MODE. With Frontispiece by E. A. Abbey. 18mo. cloth extra, gilt tops, 5*s.*

LAWSON (Right Hon. Mr. Justice)— HYMNI USITATI LATINE REDDITI, with other Verses. Small 8vo. parchment, 5*s.*

LESSING'S NATHAN THE WISE. Translated by Eustace K. Corbett. Crown 8vo. 6*s.*

LIFE THOUGHTS. Small crown 8vo. 2*s.*6*d.*

LIVING ENGLISH POETS. MDCCCLXXXII. With Frontispiece by Walter Crane. Second Edition. Large crown 8vo. printed on hand-made paper. Parchment, or cloth, 12*s.* ; vellum, 15*s.*

LOCKER (F.)—LONDON LYRICS. New Edition, with Portrait. 18mo. cloth extra, gilt tops, 5*s.*

LOVE IN IDLENESS. A Volume of Poems. With an etching by W. B. Scott. Small crown 8vo. 5*s.*

LOVE SONNETS OF PROTEUS. With Frontispiece by the Author. Elzevir 8vo. 5*s.*

LUMSDEN (Lieut.-Col. H. W.)—BEOWULF : an Old English Poem. Translated into Modern Rhymes. Second and revised Edition. Small crown 8vo. 5*s.*

LYRE AND STAR. Poems by the Author of 'Ginevra,' &c. Crown 8vo. 5*s.*

MACGREGOR (Duncan)—CLOUDS AND SUNLIGHT. Poems. Small crown 8vo. 5*s.*

MAGNUSSON (Eirikr) M.A., and PALMER (E. H.) M.A.—JOHAN LUDVIG RUNEBERG'S LYRICAL SONGS, IDYLLS, AND EPIGRAMS. Fcp. 8vo. 5*s.*

MDC. Chronicles of Christopher Columbus. A Poem in Twelve Cantos. Small crown 8vo. 7*s.* 6*d.*

MEREDITH (Owen) [*The Earl of Lytton*] LUCILE. New Edition. With 32 Illustrations. 16mo. 3*s.* 6*d.* ; cloth extra, gilt edges, 4*s.* 6*d.*

MORRIS (Lewis) — POETICAL WORKS. New and Cheaper Editions, with Portrait, complete in 3 vols. 5*s.* each.

Vol. I. contains Songs of Two Worlds. Tenth Edition.

Vol. II. contains The Epic of Hades. Seventeenth Edition.

Vol. III. contains Gwen and the Ode of Life. Sixth Edition.

THE EPIC OF HADES. With 16 Autotype Illustrations after the drawings by the late George R. Chapman. 4to. cloth extra, gilt leaves, 21*s.*

THE EPIC OF HADES. Presentation Edition. 4to. cloth extra, gilt leaves, 10*s.* 6*d.*

SONGS UNSUNG. Fourth Edition. Fcp. 8vo. 6*s.*

THE LEWIS MORRIS BIRTHDAY BOOK. Edited by S. S. Copeman. With Frontispiece after a design by the late George R. Chapman. 32mo. cloth extra, gilt edges, 2*s.* ; cloth limp, 1*s.* 6*d.*

MORSHEAD (E. D. A.)—THE HOUSE ATREUS. Being the Agamemnon, Libation-Bearers, and Furies of Æschylus. Translated into English Verse. Crown 8vo. 7*s.*

THE SUPPLIANT MAIDENS OF ÆSCHYLUS. Crown 8vo. 3s. 6d.

NADEN (Constance W.)—SONGS AND SONNETS OF SPRING TIME. Small crown 8vo. 5s.

NEWELL (E. J.)—THE SORROW OF SIMONA, and Lyrical Verses. Small crown 8vo. 3s. 6d.

NOEL (The Hon. Roden)—A LITTLE CHILD'S MONUMENT. Third Edition. Small crown 8vo. 3s. 6d.

THE RED FLAG, and other Poems. New Edition. Small crown 8vo. 6s.

O'HAGAN (John) – THE SONG OF ROLAND. Translated into English Verse. New and Cheaper Edition. Crown 8vo. 5s.

PFEIFFER (Emily)—THE RHYME OF THE LADY OF THE ROCK AND HOW IT GREW. Small crown 8vo. 3s. 6d.

GERARD'S MONUMENT, and other Poems. Second Edition. Crown 8vo. 6s.

UNDER THE ASPENS: Lyrical and Dramatic. With Portrait. Crown 8vo. 6s.

PIATT (J. J.)—IDYLS AND LYRICS OF THE OHIO VALLEY. Crown 8vo. 5s.

RAFFALOVICH (Mark André)—CYRIL AND LIONEL, and other Poems. A Volume of Sentimental Studies. Small crown 8vo. 3s. 6d.

RARE POEMS OF THE 16TH AND 17TH CENTURIES. Edited by W. J. Linton. Crown 8vo. 5s.

RHOADES (James)—THE GEORGICS OF VIRGIL. Translated into English Verse. Small crown 8vo. 5s.

ROBINSON (A. Mary F.)—A HANDFUL OF HONEYSUCKLE. Fcp. 8vo. 3s. 6d.

THE CROWNED HIPPOLYTUS. Translated from Euripides. With New Poems. Small crown 8vo. cloth, 5s.

ROUS (Lieut.-Col.)—CONRADIN. Small crown 8vo. 2s.

SCHILLER'S MARY STUART. German Text with English Translation on opposite page. By Leedham White. Crown 8vo. 6s.

SCOTT (E. J. L.)—THE ECLOGUES OF VIRGIL. Translated into English Verse. Small crown 8vo. 3s. 6d.

SCOTT (George F. E.)—THEODORA, and other Poems. Small crown 8vo. 3s. 6d.

SEAL (W. H.) — IONE, and other Poems. Second and cheaper edition, revised, crown 8vo. 3s. 6d.

SELKIRK (J. B.)—POEMS. Crown 8vo. 7s. 6d.

SHARP (William) — EUPHRENIA; or, The Test of Love. A Poem. Crown 8vo. 5s.

SKINNER (H. J.)—THE LILY OF THE LYN, and other Poems. Small crown 8vo. 3s. 6d.

SLADEN (Douglas B. W.)—FRITHJOF AND INGEBJORG, and other Poems. Small crown 8vo. 5s.

SMITH (J. W. Gilbart)—THE LOVES OF VANDYCK: a Tale of Genoa. Small crown 8vo. 2s. 6d.

THE LOG O' THE 'NORSEMAN,' Small crown 8vo. 5s.

SOPHOCLES: The Seven Plays in English Verse. Translated by Lewis Campbell. Crown 8vo. 7s. 6d.

SPICER (Henry)—HASKA: a Drama in Three Acts (as represented at the Theatre Royal, Drury Lane, March 10th, 1877). Third Edition, crown 8vo. 3s. 6d.

SYMONDS (John Addington) — VAGABUNDULI LIBELLUS. Crown 8vo. 6s.

TARES. Crown 8vo. 1s. 6d.

TASSO'S JERUSALEM DELIVERED. Translated by Sir John Kingston James, Bart. 2 vols. printed on hand-made paper, parchment, bevelled boards, large crown 8vo. 21s.

TAYLOR (Sir H.)—Works Complete in Five Volumes. Crown 8vo. 30s.

PHILIP VAN ARTEVELDE. Fcp. 8vo. 3s. 6d.

THE VIRGIN WIDOW, &c. Fcp. 8vo. 3s. 6d.

THE STATESMAN. Fcp. 8vo. 3s. 6d.

TAYLOR (Augustus) — POEMS. Fcp. 8vo. 5s.

TAYLOR (*Margaret Scott*) — 'BOYS TOGETHER,' and other Poems. Small crown 8vo. 6s.

THORNTON (*L. M.*)—THE SON OF SHELOMITH. Small crown 8vo. 3s. 6d.

TODHUNTER (*Dr. J.*) — LAURELLA, and other Poems. Crown 8vo. 6s. 6d.

FOREST SONGS. Small crown 8vo. 3s. 6d.

THE TRUE TRAGEDY OF RIENZI: a Drama. Crown 8vo. 3s. 6d.

ALCESTIS: a Dramatic Poem. Extra fcp. 8vo. 5s.

TYLER (*M. C.*) — ANNE BOLEYN: a Tragedy in Six Acts. Small crown 8vo. 2s. 6d.

WALTERS (*Sophia Lydia*) — A DREAMER'S SKETCH BOOK. With 21 Illustrations by Percival Skelton, R. P. Leitch, W. H. J. Boot, and T. R. Pritchett. Engraved by J. D. Cooper. Fcp. 4to. 12s. 6d.

WANDERING ECHOES. By J. E. D. G. In Four Parts. Small crown 8vo. 5s.

WATTS (*Alaric Alfred and Emma Mary Howitt*) — AURORA: a Medley of Verse. Fcp. 8vo. cloth, bevelled boards, 5s.

WEBSTER (*Augusta*)—IN A DAY: a Drama. Small crown 8vo. 2s. 6d.

DISGUISES: a Drama. Small crown 8vo. 5s.

WET DAYS. By a Farmer. Small crown 8vo. 6s.

WILLIAMS (*J.*)—A STORY OF THREE YEARS, and other Poems. Small crown 8vo. 3s. 6d.

WORDSWORTH BIRTHDAY BOOK, THE. Edited by ADELAIDE and VIOLET WORDSWORTH. 32mo. limp cloth, 1s. 6d.; cloth extra, 2s.

YOUNGMAN (*Thomas George*)—POEMS. Small crown 8vo. 5s.

YOUNGS (*Ella Sharpe*)—PAPHUS, and other Poems. Small crown 8vo. 3s. 6d.

A HEARTS LIFE, SARPEDON, and other Poems. Small crown 8vo. 3s. 6d.

WORKS OF FICTION IN ONE VOLUME.

BANKS (*Mrs. G. L.*)—GOD'S PROVIDENCE HOUSE. New Edition. Crown 8vo. 3s. 6d.

HUNTER (*Hay*)—CRIME OF CHRISTMAS DAY. A Tale of the Latin Quarter. By the Author of 'My Ducats and My Daughter.' 1s.

HUNTER (*Hay*) *and WHYTE* (*Walter*) MY DUCATS AND MY DAUGHTER. New and Cheaper Edition. With Frontispiece. Crown 8vo. 6s.

INGELOW (*Jean*)—OFF THE SKELLIGS. A Novel. With Frontispiece. Second Edition. Crown 8vo. 6s.

KIELLAND (*Alexander L.*)—GARMAN AND WORSE. A Norwegian Novel. Authorised Translation by W. W. Kettlewell. Crown 8vo. 6s.

MACDONALD (*G.*)—DONAL GRANT. A Novel. New and Cheap Edition, with Frontispiece. Crown 8vo. 6s.

CASTLE WARLOCK. A Novel. New and Cheaper Edition. Crown 8vo. 9s.

MALCOLM. With Portrait of the Author engraved on Steel. Sixth Edition. Crown 8vo. 6s.

THE MARQUIS OF LOSSIE. Fifth Edition. With Frontispiece. Crown 8vo. 6s.

ST. GEORGE AND ST. MICHAEL. Fourth Edition. With Frontispiece. Crown 8vo. 6s.

PALGRAVE (*W. Gifford*)—HERMANN AGHA: an Eastern Narrative. Third Edition. Crown 8vo. 6s.

SHAW (*Flora L.*)—CASTLE BLAIR; a Story of Youthful Days. New and Cheaper Edition. Crown 8vo. 3s. 6d.

STRETTON (*Hesba*) — THROUGH A NEEDLE'S EYE. A Story. New and Cheaper Edition, with Frontispiece. Crown 8vo. 6s.

TAYLOR (*Col. Meadows*) *C.S.I., M.R.I.A.*

SEETA. A Novel. New and Cheaper Edition. With Frontispiece. Crown 8vo. 6s.

TIPPOO SULTAUN: a Tale of the Mysore War. New Edition, with Frontispiece. Crown 8vo. 6s.

RALPH DARNELL. New and Cheaper Edition. With Frontispiece. Crown 8vo. 6s.

C

TAYLOR—continued.
A NOBLE QUEEN. New and Cheaper Edition. With Frontispiece. Crown 8vo. 6s.
THE CONFESSIONS OF A THUG. Crown 8vo. 6s.

TAYLOR—continued.
TARA: a Mahratta Tale. Crown 8vo. 6s.
WITHIN SOUND OF THE SEA. New and Cheaper Edition, with Frontispiece. Crown 8vo. 6s.

BOOKS FOR THE YOUNG.

BRAVE MEN'S FOOTSTEPS. A Book of Example and Anecdote for Young People. By the Editor of 'Men who have Risen.' With Four Illustrations by C. Doyle. Eighth Edition. Crown 8vo. 3s. 6d.

COXHEAD (Ethel)—BIRDS AND BABIES. With 33 Illustrations. Imp. 16mo. cloth gilt, 2s. 6d.

DAVIES (G. Christopher) — RAMBLES AND ADVENTURES OF OUR SCHOOL FIELD CLUB. With Four Illustrations. New and Cheaper Edition. Crown 8vo. 3s. 6d.

EDMONDS (Herbert) — WELL-SPENT LIVES: a Series of Modern Biographies. New and Cheaper Edition. Crown 8vo. 3s. 6d.

EVANS (Mark)—THE STORY OF OUR FATHER'S LOVE, told to Children. Sixth and Cheaper Edition of Theology for Children. With Four Illustrations. Fcp. 8vo. 1s. 6d.

JOHNSON (Virginia W.)—THE CATSKILL FAIRIES. Illustrated by ALFRED FREDERICKS. 5s.

MAC KENNA (S. J.)—PLUCKY FELLOWS. A Book for Boys. With Six Illustrations. Fifth Edition. Crown 8vo. 3s. 6d.

REANEY (Mrs. G. S.)—WAKING AND WORKING; or, From Girlhood to Womanhood. New and Cheaper Edition. With a Frontispiece. Cr. 8vo. 3s. 6d.

BLESSING AND BLESSED: a Sketch of Girl Life. New and Cheaper Edition. Crown 8vo. 3s. 6d.

REANEY (Mrs. G. S.)—continued.
ROSE GURNEY'S DISCOVERY. A Book for Girls. Dedicated to their Mothers. Crown 8vo. 3s. 6d.

ENGLISH GIRLS: Their Place and Power. With Preface by the Rev. R. W. Dale. Fourth Edition. Fcp. 8vo. 2s. 6d.

JUST ANYONE, and other Stories. Three Illustrations. Royal 16mo. 1s. 6d.

SUNBEAM WILLIE, and other Stories. Three Illustrations. Royal 16mo. 1s. 6d.

SUNSHINE JENNY, and other Stories. Three Illustrations. Royal 16mo. 1s. 6d.

STOCKTON (Frank R.)—A JOLLY FELLOWSHIP. With 20 Illustrations. Crown 8vo. 5s.

STORR (Francis) and TURNER (Hawes). CANTERBURY CHIMES; or, Chaucer Tales Re-told to Children. With Six Illustrations from the Ellesmere MS. Third Edition. Fcp. 8vo. 3s. 6d.

STRETTON (Hesba)—DAVID LLOYD'S LAST WILL. With Four Illustrations. New Edition. Royal 16mo. 2s. 6d.

TALES FROM ARIOSTO RE-TOLD FOR CHILDREN. By a Lady. With Three Illustrations. Crown 8vo. 4s. 6d.

WHITAKER (Florence)—CHRISTY'S INHERITANCE: A London Story. Illustrated. Royal 16mo. 1s. 6d.

LONDON: PRINTED BY
SPOTTISWOODE AND CO., NEW-STREET SQUARE
AND PARLIAMENT STREET

www.ingramcontent.com/pod-product-compliance
Lightning Source LLC
Chambersburg PA
CBHW020804230426
43666CB00007B/843